The Heart of Counseling

Discovering and Embracing
Your Authentic Self as a Therapist

By

Michelle Engblom-Deglmann

Published by hope*books
2217 Matthews Township Pkwy
Suite D302
Matthews, NC 28105
www.hopebooks.com

hope*books is a division of hope*media

Printed in the United States of America

First paperback edition.

Paperback ISBN: 979-8-89185-066-8
Hardcover ISBN: 979-8-89185-067-5
Ebook ISBN: 979-8-89185-068-2
Library of Congress Number: 2024931112

hope*books
hopebooks.com

PRAISE FOR
The Heart of Counseling

Dr. Engblom-Deglmann's book will be reassuring and encouraging to young therapists. She offers beginners understanding and permission to trust themselves. Much of the training of graduate students is academic, but this book provides therapists with an education in the heart. I recommend it for all beginning therapists.

MARY PIPHER, PhD, author of 11 books including
Letters to a Young Therapist and Four-time New York Times
bestselling books including *Reviving Ophelia*

Reading *The Heart of Counseling* feels like curling up under the blanket and taking a break from the stress and overwhelm that is so often mental health training and practice. My soul felt like it took a deep exhale and soaked up profound truths from a wise and gentle teacher. Dr. Michelle masterfully walks the line of being warm, challenging, engaging and relevant. I felt deeply understood and pointedly challenged from the first page. This inspiring book belongs in the hands of any therapist who believes their work, and the field in general, deserves more heart.

SEAN DAVIS, PhD, LMFT, Distinguished Professor,
Alliant International University Co-author of
Family Therapy: Concepts and Methods

The Heart of Counseling captures the voice of an experienced mentor guiding therapists-in-training to become their genuine selves. Dr. Engblom-Deglmann communicates in an intimate, trustworthy and, at times, vulnerable way to normalize and engage those learning the art of clinical work. Offering many examples of early career fears as well as offering exercises to flourish, this book will be a reliable companion in your professional clinical journey.

CLAUDIA GRAUF-GROUNDS, PhD, LMFT Professor Emerita Marriage & Family Therapy, Seattle Pacific University Author of *Essential Skills in Family Therapy, A Practice Beyond Cultural Humility*

This is the book I wish I'd had as a new therapist 30 years ago. In a masterful way, Dr. Michelle shares clinically sound wisdom, encouragement, and guidance that provides a roadmap through the maze of confusion that often overwhelms beginners to the counseling field. *The Heart of Counseling* will inspire every reader to bring their authentic self to the therapeutic process while trusting that individual uniqueness is a beautiful gift to the world.

MICHELLE WATSON CANFIELD, PhD, LPC Author of *Let's Talk: Conversation Starters for Dads and Daughters* Podcast host, The Dad Whisperer

Michelle is both the wise sage and kind friend all therapists need for this unique career. This book is a transformative guide for any therapist, masterfully blending professional wisdom with personal growth. It touches the heart of counseling, encouraging us to embrace our authentic and vulnerable parts of us as our greatest strength. Michelle will call forth the best and most beautiful part of you. And in your darkest moments she is beside you saying, "Me too, you are not alone."

TRISTEN COLLINS, MA, LPC Co-author of *Why Emotions Matter*

Leaning into her own personal and professional journey, Dr. Engblom-Deglmann has masterfully written a book that creates space for the reader to do the same. Authentic, reflective, vulnerable, humorous, poignant, educational and hopeful. Whether a beginning therapist or seasoned professional, *The*

Heart of Counseling will teach or remind you why we do this work in the first place, because of the transformation that comes via authentic relationships.

RICHARD SHAW, D.MFT, LMFT, LMHC Associate Professor
of Marriage & Family Therapy, George Fox University Author of
Shame No More: A Framework for Healing through Grace.

Dr. Michelle is the mentor you always wanted as a new counselor. Bringing her decades of experience and expertise with clients and training new therapists, she has written a book that needs to be every growing counselor's closest companion. Dr. Michelle's wisdom, vulnerability, and ability to put to words what every counselor is wrestling with and pondering at the end of the day, will make you laugh, cry, and become more fully confident in your own skin.

TERRA MATTSON, MA LMFT, LPC Author of Courageous:
Being Daughters Rooted in Grace and Co-author of
Shrinking the Integrity Gap; Co-founder of Courageous Girls

This is a powerful book with a big heart. I encourage new masters students and experienced psychotherapists to read this book. Every therapist should encounter the deep, caring, moving descriptions Michelle provides of the emotional journey of the developing and practicing psychotherapist. This book is an outstanding exploration of the emotional challenges faced by every therapist.

DOUG PETTINELLI, PhD, LMFT Former Professor of
Family and Community Medicine, St. Louis University

The Heart of Counseling is an important book that promotes the power of self for the academically trained student. Dr. Michelle gives us permission to bring our heart with us into our education and career. As a mentor and author, she magically attunes to our vulnerabilities to reimagine them as pathways to success. Her words are poetic and filled with love, compassion and grit reflecting her teaching style in writing. She has gifted us with a path to unearth our authentic selves.

NANCY SALISBURY, MD, MFT Associate

This book is something I can easily picture myself picking up again and again, on the many Day Ones still to come for me (first day in Practicum, first day seeing clients, first day out of Grad School...). While written like an encouraging letter from a mentor, it provides practical solutions on how to manage feelings of imposter syndrome as well as ways to stay authentic to yourself in your role as a therapist.

SAMMI HARVEY, Graduate Student,
George Fox University

This book is dedicated to you, dear counselor.

To the students, interns, colleagues, and counselors who have taught me so much and contributed to the contents of this book throughout my time as a counselor and professor.

These words are a gift from you and for you.

May you always be inspired to bring your authentic self to your work as a counselor.

. . . .

Thank you to my dad, whose artistic talents grace the illustrations of this book, enriching its content with his unique style and authenticity.

Foreword

I have loved being involved in counselor education and supervision for nearly three decades. It is a privilege to contribute to educational materials, especially related to Emotionally Focused Therapy (EFT) given my roles as a Certified EFT Trainer and Supervisor.

When Michelle approached me about *The Heart of Counseling* and her desire to support counselors to engage with presence and authenticity, I was genuinely delighted. As therapists, it is vital we learn how to connect with our clients authentically, utilizing our empathy and warmth.

Authenticity is at the core of effective therapy. Each week I consult with therapists worldwide who are dedicated to honing their skills and presence to positively impact their clients' lives. Michelle's book serves as a guide to help you understand and enhance your use of self, enabling you to bring your genuine care, courage, and heart to your therapeutic work. She hopes that you can be your true self and an effective therapist at the same time. This aspect is often overlooked in graduate programs and counselor development, making Michelle's contribution invaluable.

I first crossed paths with Michelle in 2012 during an EFT training I conducted in San Francisco. She was a Clinical Training Director and therapist then and has since become a highly accomplished professor. *The Heart of Counseling: Discovering and*

Embracing your Authentic Self as a Therapist is a topic that resonates deeply with Michelle because she embodies it in her own life.

Michelle and I share a commitment to lifelong learning and professional development. She consistently demonstrates authenticity, warmth, and engagement in her interactions. She knows her heart. She speaks her heart. Through her book, you'll come to know her heart, and in doing so you'll find the courage to be vulnerable and connected to yourself and your clients – a crucial aspect because connection is the center of meaningful experience and supports the creation of meaningful change.

The Heart of Counseling guides you through the journey of exploring different facets of your heart and its essential role in your therapeutic relationships. The section titles - *Burdened, Becoming, Belonging* -capture the essence of this journey, flowing like a gentle stream traveling to increasingly beautiful territory. Every step of this journey matters deeply.

As therapists, we carry burdens - our own concerns and fears - while we support others in their healing and growth. Michelle skillfully unveils these common burdens therapists face and guides us to embrace them, recognizing the beauty and authenticity within them to enhance our connection with clients.

Michelle effortlessly combines her teaching expertise with authenticity in her writing. She draws us into the journey with real-life examples, poignant prose, powerful quotes, and the use of her own lived experiences, making the effectiveness of authenticity palpable and accessible.

With her background as a counselor educator who embodies authenticity in her work and life, Michelle is the perfect guide on this journey. She gently leads you to find your heart at home in authenticity.

While much of our training as therapists focuses on rules, regulations, ethics, and skills – all crucial elements - our inner world, particularly our hearts, often receives less attention. However, it is in our hearts that true connection resides. Through *The Heart of Counseling*, you'll discover how to live in connection and be your authentic self with your clients.

Rebecca Jorgensen, PhD

EFT Trainer and Supervisor

Contents

INTRODUCTION

Here's the Deal

I n the process of writing this book, I would sometimes reach out to current and former students and pose questions to dig into their experiences as new counselors. As a professor and a licensed counselor for over 20 years, sometimes it's hard to be in the mindset and mental space of what it feels like to be a beginner. One day in particular, I reached out to about 20 current and former students and asked them about the specific statements that go through their heads when they feel worthless as a counselor. Usually, when I ask them these "book questions," I get responses over the next week as they ponder and then respond or forget to respond. However, this question, "What do you say to yourself when you feel worthless as a counselor," brought an instant flurry of responses.

Excited to read their replies, I began opening the messages, eager to use the information to connect with you, my reader. Then I started reading message after message and began to cry. I cried tears of thanksgiving for their vulnerability. I cried tears of pain for these messages. I cried tears of feeling seen by people who don't even know my story. I cried tears of feeling known—known in my own feelings of insecurity and pain. Places I thought nobody else could see. But their words speak to all of us, to you and to me, in places where we have deep desires to do things well, but our fears speak things like...

I'm a fraud
Why would you think anyone would want you as their therapist?
What do you know?
Why did I even think I could do this?

I'm not doing enough
I'm not enough for my clients
Someone else could be doing a better job for this client than I am

I'm too broken
I'm too sensitive
People don't respect a fat therapist

I'm not competent
I don't know what I'm doing
I'm not skilled enough to help this client

The honesty and raw vulnerability in these messages brought me to tears. In a matter of two hours, I received *over a hundred* statements just like these. Over one hundred statements that we roll through our brains that tell us to stop doing this work because we aren't worthy, or old enough, or smart enough or _____ enough. And they not only scroll through our heads but also run deep through our hearts. And they take up residence there in those safe yet vulnerable spaces. And they sure do settle in, don't they? Because they settle in and unpack themselves in the rooms of our hearts, they are easy for us to access. No matter how hard we try to battle these messages, they are right there, settled in, ready to jump at any hint of insecurity. What on earth do I have to offer? Why did I think I could even do this?

As I sit here writing these words and reflecting on the experience of receiving these messages and these reminders, I feel it deeply. This experience right here, of receiving easily-accessible messages fighting against our worth as counselors, is the very reason this book was created. The purpose. The message. The goal. The why. These messages that float around in our minds are such a crucial part of the unpacking and learning process in becoming a counselor.

But in our academic training, nobody tends to these messages that underlie our learning and growing process. Our professors and supervisors want to know we are learning, and they pour into our brain. But who tends to our hearts? Who searches the depths of our hearts and nurtures the health of our root systems? In my experience...nobody. Not one professor taught me how to tend to these statements of doubt and self-loathing and fear and vulnerability and brokenness. Nobody taught me the most important part of our work is being *with* people and loving people well. Nobody taught me that the actual foundation, the heart of the work of a counselor, is the very heart of the counselor. So I'm here to do that for you and with you, dear reader. I'm here to show up and remind you, share with you, and invite you to do that work with me, as I have done with hundreds before you. Because, reader, your heart is worth being nurtured. Yes, yours.

This book was created from my heart to yours to help you be more like you.

Quite simply, I don't think you need to change who you are. This book wasn't written to help you be more like me or like counseling theorists or like your professors or supervisors. This book wasn't written to tell you how to sit, what to say, how to pick a theory, or how to squeeze yourself into a pre-made mold of what it means to be a therapist. This book was created from my heart to yours to help you be more like you. To give you permission to be more like you. To fully invite you to be more like you, inside the counseling room and outside of the counseling room. I think you are already brilliant, and my hope is to remind you of that, not to change you. I want to uncover the layers, not add to the learning. My invitation to you is for you to get to know yourself, just as you are right here. Right in that gray space of growing, of not knowing, of wondering, needing, searching, seeking, and longing.

And as you are doing that, I know it often feels scary and unsettling. I know finding your way and discovering your authentic self feels like a big task. I know. It was and is a big task for me, too. As a beginning counselor, it was scary and lonely. In my process of learning how to be a writer for you, it was scary and lonely. I so desperately want the pages of this book to be an intentional process of undoing aloneness. To walk hand in hand with you along this path and share with you:

Who you are is already enough
I see you
I am you
And you are not alone.

I've created a pathway here, in these pages, to undo the aloneness that can come in this field. When doubts creep in.

When imposter syndrome clouds you. When your own broken-ness feels like a lot. When you feel lost. When you feel burdened. You are not alone. I've worn a pathway here for us to travel together through the forest. My deep desire for you, reader, in these pages, is to help you find your path. And what I hope for is a redefined place of "I've arrived." What if the place we're going together is not arriving at all? What if we stop focusing on the **burden** of the destination and start living in the spaces where we're learning and growing and **becoming** and **belonging**? Right where we are. Right where you are, reader. Right there.

Because here's the deal: I believe you know why you want to become a therapist—a really good one that makes a differ-ence in people's lives. I believe you are trying hard to do your own work while also helping others. I believe that the more you learn, the less prepared you feel to sit with others. But I believe in you because I've seen you change and learn and grow and begin to believe in yourself. Maybe not you, exactly, but hun-dreds of others just like you who have gone before you and doubted, feared, hidden, and *overcome*. They found themselves in the process of learning how to do this work that was deeply hidden behind and under the hundreds of layers of books and papers and presentations. It was there before you started, and it's still there now. Coax it out...your passion is there.

I believe in you. Yes, I know. I haven't met you, but it's true—I do believe in you. I know I don't know your story, I don't know how broken you are, I don't know the content of your nightmares or how strong you have imposter syndrome every day. But I believe you have found the field of counseling with great purpose and intention. Let's discover or rediscover it together, and let's nurture it. Let's nurture your desire to help from who you were created to be. Let's nurture your truths that are hidden behind fears. Let's nurture your confidence that was there before you started. Let's nurture the curiosity for people that brought you to this field in the first place. Let's believe, together, that you are called here to this place of being a counselor, and let's rediscover your passion for health, for healing, for love, compassion, growing, and honoring and strengthening relationships. Let me welcome you, *fully you*, to the calling of being a counselor.

Take my hand by way of these pages as we seek to find the pathway from

I'm not enough
I'm too broken
I'm a fraud
I'm scared

To the place of

I am enough
I am worthy
There's beautiful in broken
My full self matters
I belong here

Those beautiful people who shared with me their fears? They also shared with me their inherent words of worth—by the hundreds. The words that dance alongside the other words. The words that were born out of learning and growing. There's a way for you, too, here; there's a pathway from burdened to becoming to belonging. It was there all along—it's in you. It is you. And it is the heart of counseling.

PART ONE

Burdened

*"Sometimes when you're in a dark place you think you've been **buried**, but you've actually been **planted**."*

Christine Caine[1]

CHAPTER ONE

Buried Under Books

❝ Why are you here?" was the sentence written on the white-board of my Introduction to Marriage and Family Therapy course as I taught the first day of class. Students in the program lovingly call this course the "theory class" due to the endless list of theories to be covered in the sixteen-week course. We cover all the basics: narrative, solution-focused, structural, Bowenian, and then squeeze in all the important other ones as well: Internal Family Systems, Emotionally Focused Therapy, Acceptance and Commitment Therapy. And for most students, it is one of the first classes they take in their graduate school program. I invited the group of twenty-two students to come up to the board and share the first thing that came into their minds when they read the question scrawled across the board: "Why are you here?" As students looked around the room at each other, a few hesitantly approached the board and began to write, and a theme quickly emerged.

It's required
It's on my best route plan
To become an MFT
To learn about theories
Because my academic advisor told me to

We quietly gazed at the responses together, wondering. After a moment passed, I asked them again and emphasized a particular word by erasing the word "why" and replacing it in all uppercase letters, "WHY are you here?" I let the silence linger, and as I looked across the room, I saw their whole beings soften. Their tight shoulders began to relax. Their bouncing legs stopped. The desperation to get the answer right evaporated. This was not a question that had a right or wrong answer. This was something inside of them. I saw the students move from eager theory learners to humans. I could see lightness spread across the room; a collective togetherness sprung out of their souls. It was almost as if they yearned to be asked this question. This time, more students engaged on the whiteboard and shared:

To help the hurting
Add tools to my toolbox
To learn how to help people well
To love
Hold people in their pain and suffering
Be a voice for those too scared to speak
Trauma
I am called to do this work

Ah, yes. There, scrawled across the board, was the important *why*. The personal, the instrumental, the creative, called, genuine and can't-get-this-answer-wrong responses. These answers matter a great deal. Graduate school can hide our why. Graduate school can suffocate our creativity. It can stifle our uniqueness. Graduate school can be detrimental to our growing process. There, I said it.

Graduate school can be detrimental to our growing process.

In learning to become a counselor, it's easy to lose our own voice, our uniqueness, and our authenticity. In the learning process, it's so easy to lose our grasp on why we entered this field in the first place—your *why*. Everyone has a *why* story...the one you get asked on graduate school applications: "Why do you want to become a counselor?" We all have a story of what brought us to this field. For some of us, it's our own experiences from our past when someone, perhaps even a counselor, stepped into our lives and helped us work through those circumstances. We felt inspired, supported, and listened to, and we decided at some point we wanted to offer that to others going through tough experiences.

For others, we were left without anyone to process through our struggles, loneliness, confusion, and lack of sufficient support. And that leaves us with a desire to be that person for others, to be the person we didn't have in our lives. Everyone has a reason for wanting to become a counselor. We didn't land in this field by accident. We are here with great intention. Do you remember what your *why* is? Or is it a fleeting thought that slips through your grasp while learning *how* to become that helper you want to become?

While graduate school is filled with amazing learning opportunities, it can often become a slippery slope from "Oh, I'm actually going to school to become a counselor!" to "Oh my Lord, what was I thinking—I can't do this!" This slide from our heart, our intent, and our purpose to our head, where we focus on learning all the things, is natural. It happens for most people. And it's severe. We get buried under the various aspects of learning and nurturing our brains. We become so buried that we lose our way in the mess of learning.

Buried Under Books

I believe, for most of us, the more you learn, the less prepared you feel to sit with others as a counselor. I believe this is a necessary part of the learning and growing experience, as unfortunate as it is. I believe the more books we read, the more theories we learn, and the more clinical skills we rehearse, we become closer to and further from our ultimate goal of sitting with people in their pain. The learning part is important and serves an important function. And the learning part fills our brains but doesn't fill our hearts.

As a mental health professional, you spend a great deal of time learning. You learn counseling skills and practice them in role-plays with peers. You pore over books and papers and exams in an effort to learn as much as you can about how to sit with clients. Don't get me wrong—this learning is important and crucial work; it supplies us with necessary skills and ethical guidelines. I'm not advocating that we don't learn the necessary skills. I'm not advocating that we don't take all the coursework and spend the time learning and reading and writing and regurgitating information. As a professor, I hope it's obvious that I significantly value the learning and growing process. It is essential we learn about mental health diagnoses, ethical decision-making models, theoretical orientations, and all the courses and learning outcomes mapped out for you in your syllabi. This learning gives us a roadmap for how we do this work.

This learning, though, is cognitive, focused, academic, head-space learning. While this is a foundational part of a mental health practitioner's development, it's only part of the story. While necessary and essential, this academic learning can also prevent us from sinking into our hearts and connecting with clients from that space. And as counselors, we need both. Some programs place a lot of emphasis on the personal growth required to be a counselor as well, and I applaud those programs. Other programs work so hard to meet various accreditation standards and curriculum requirements that they leave no room to focus on the heart of counseling. We need academic learning to strengthen our brains and inform our decisions, and we need heart-space learning: discovering and growing and even unlearning in ways that nurture our hearts in addition to our minds. We get so caught up in thinking about the next question we should ask when sitting with clients that we forget to listen, to be curious, to relate with and feel what the client is sharing with us. And these spaces are what create the heart of counseling.

> Academic learning focuses on the head. And while that's important, it's only half of the story.

Our hearts need to be held, too. Our hearts need to learn how to hold hard spaces. Our hearts need to learn how to not let the trauma of others sink into our vulnerable spaces. Our hearts need to hear that we are enough. We are already created to be in these spaces with others. We already have what it takes. The academic learning parts are essential extras in an already prepared soul.

Buried Under Expectations

Shuttling from this academic head space to the more intimate heart space requires us to let go of the idea of what a counselor "should" look like. Sometimes while working with students, I see them get so worried about what a therapist looks like, acts like, and sounds like. The expectations are so high around this perception of how we're supposed to show up as therapists in the therapy room. To challenge students around these perceptions, I encourage students to pretend the client and themselves are sitting in a coffee shop, or to pretend it's a mom at school pick up or the school fundraiser, or to think of the person as another dad at a sporting event. While these examples can introduce all kinds of boundary and ethical issues, they invite us to think of counseling as less scripted and robotic and more of a loving and supportive conversation. Just this slight change in how we think about the process of counseling can help students relax into the heart space a bit more, just one human with another human, not one expert, all-knowing, fully-arrived counselor with a client.

Picture, for a moment, what a typical counselor looks like. Picture how they sit, the words they use, the movements of their bodies, the phrases they say, and the brilliance they bring to the room. Do you have the image in your mind?

What do you see? I think many of us see clean-cut, articulate, poised, stoic, unphased, clinical (detached?), analytical, and thoughtful professionals. Many of us believe that counselors sit a certain way, use certain phrases, and exude a certain "clinical" presence. You know what? I think this is total garbage, and this persona is as likely to hurt the therapeutic relationship as help it. In this learning process of how to become a counselor, it's important to understand that what we bring to the table matters. We can easily get so overwhelmed by all the instructors and voices and textbooks and papers and theorists informing us what we *should* do that it's easy to stop shuttling to our hearts to find our own voices. Those voices can become incredibly overwhelming, and we shut down and shut out our own voices and instead rely on the voices of "others."

Recently, a student I teach shared with me that "for much of the first year of this program, I was under the impression that I had to turn off aspects of myself and put on the hat of a therapist." It took me longer than I care to admit to learn this is incredibly inaccurate. Rather than this image of what a counselor should look like, I started to imagine a space that looked different. I imagined a safe space filled with compassion, warmth, safety, and relaxation for me and my clients.

It took me years in my career to see that the perfectionist parts of me were not being served by examples of master therapists doing their art with such skill, absent of flaws or missteps. It took me longer than I care to admit, but I will let you into that space, reader, in hopes it takes you just a little bit less. It took me over ten years to learn that what the masters don't show you—and what I experience nearly every session—is quite normal. Part of this work is getting confused, feeling lost, not tracking the client, disagreeing with the client, feeling stuck, feeling overwhelmed, having my heart tugged on, and feeling like a big, humongous imposter. The world will miss out on the most valuable gifts we have to offer if we pretend to be this ideal counselor.

Buried Under Theory

Those "master" therapists often show theories flawlessly executed and make the rest of us counselors feel like theory is the ultimate thing for us to master. And theory is important, but what beginners often get buried under is the integration of theory.

Theory is much more about providing a map of where you are going, but how you get there and the vehicle you take is unique to each individual counselor.

In academia, students are often encouraged to "pick a theory." To me, this feels a lot like asking a new high school graduate to "declare their major" when they have no clue what college or a career even looks like yet. When I was completing my master's degree, we wrote a lengthy and culminating capstone paper and had to apply a particular theory to a particular client. I picked Cognitive Behavioral Therapy (CBT) because...I have no idea why. Probably because it was easy to identify the steps and stages, and it had some tangible learning applications to help me write the paper. It's a good theory; it's empirically based and works with a wide range of presenting client problems. I had the idea that this was now my theory; I was married to it, and we were destined to be together forever. I'm not sure where I got that idea, but I know I wasn't the only one.

While I started my career married to CBT, I have since expanded my view of human nature, suffering, health, and healing. And so I migrated through, even stumbled through, various theories until I found one that felt more congruent with how I felt humans change. That sifting and migrating and searching is a crucial part of the learning and growing process. Let me encourage you to change and grow and move from theory to theory until you find one that resonates with you.

The Theory Chooses You

There's a great scene in the first Harry Potter[1] movie where Harry is in the wand store trying to pick out his wand. He approaches the wand master and, with trepidation, shares:

"I still need a wand."

The wand master searches the rows of dusty shelves smattered with various wands stashed in boxes and returns and offers one to Harry. Harry tentatively picks it up, waves it, and immediately bookshelves tip over and a file cabinet bursts open, sending papers flying into the room. Clearly, that was not the wand for him. The wand master turns away and searches for another wand. "Perhaps this," he says. Harry waves the wand and glass shatters in all directions across the room. The wand master turns back to the shelves again and, seeming intentionally curious about this third wand, offers it to Harry. The moment Harry grasps the third wand, the skies part, a powerful wind blows, and the lights begin to flicker. The wand master says, "The wand chooses the wizard, Mr. Potter...It's not always clear why, and it is clear that we can expect great things from you."

Spoiler alert: once Harry finds the right wand for him—the one that is made for him—he does do great things. Like Harry Potter and his wand, a theory chooses you; you can't force the wrong one to fit. Once you begin to practice counseling, one or two theories will organically begin to flow from you, based on belief systems that you gravitate towards, without perhaps even knowing it. Once I gave myself permission to lessen my grasp on CBT and just "do counseling," I realized I asked specific questions about a client's history, how connected they are to the people who raised them, and if that influenced how they connect to others now. I leaned into the spaces where clients felt known and cared for and where their emotional needs were met. It turns out, that closely aligns with a particular theory or two, and once I connected words like "connections" to "attachments" and "emotional needs" to "emotionally focused," theory began to emerge from what I was already doing. Then, I integrated the specifics of the theory and I read up on frameworks and interventions. But first, I let the wand find me.

> The academic learning parts are essential extras in an already prepared soul.

Your theory will find you if you are open and looking. Let go of trying to force one to fit you while breaking windows and tossing bookshelves along the way. The theory will find you, and when one or two do, lean into them and let them be the map that shows you the way. There are golden threads that run through each given theory that define the main concept of change—the heart of the change process according to the given theory. Does that encapsulate what you believe about people? Does it represent how you believe change happens or your view of human health and struggle?

If you sit with someone and naturally, organically try to connect with them, you will naturally, inevitably, start to exhibit characteristics of existing theories. Someone watching you will be able to identify, "The way you're connecting with this client is really a lot like narrative therapy." Then, you can learn about it, read about it, try it on, and see how it fits. But it starts with the ways you naturally interact and learn about people, one human being to another, not by artificially trying to demonstrate a theory you don't naturally connect with. And when you start integrating theory, it won't look like the masters and original theorists; it will look like your own authentic interpretation of theory. Theory only informs who we already are and what we already have in us.

Finding Flare In Theory

Finding this authentic interpretation is true in life and in the counseling space. When my husband and I were newly married, we took a dance class together with another couple. My husband and I both grew up in the middle of nowhere Minnesota, where the only dance we did was the required and incredibly awkward dance classes in middle school and then Oktober fests jigs at the local church where all the adults dosey-doed with one another. Neither of us has a dancing bone in our bodies. We are stiff and awkward and don't especially enjoy dancing—I'm not sure we even danced at our own wedding. But we took salsa dancing lessons. Let me rephrase that: we took one. We took one salsa dancing lesson.

As soon as we walked through the door of the dance studio, we both stopped and slowly turned and looked at each other with wide eyes and a knowing glance that communicated, "We should just leave now." The lights were already low, the fast and light music was playing, and the trainers and fellow learners were already twisting and turning and flipping all over the dance floor. One of the trainers ran over to me, grabbed my hand, and coaxed me onto the dance floor with him. He started counting, his feet moving in a complicated pattern over and over. He kept counting and doing these steps. I think he assumed I would catch on; I did not catch on. I stared at his feet, so light and bouncy, and his whole body followed, all while smiling and moving his arms in a synchronous flowing pattern that confused me. How did his feet do one thing and his arms do another thing, and how was he counting? He continued, encouraging me to, "Feel the music and feel the beat," and, "Let your body flow into the sounds of the song." No, kind sir, my body doesn't do that.

I glared at my husband, who was finding this all a bit amusing. My glare said, "Get over here right this minute, grab my hand, and take me out of here now." He rescued me. We found a place in the back of the room where we spent the class making fun of ourselves, in awe of others who were catching on quickly, and not doing very much dancing. We left early, found a local restaurant, and instead of dancing the salsa, we ate the salsa. I still don't know much about salsa, except it's delicious on chips. But I do know that there is a clearly defined structure (which makes my heart happy) and then a lot of flamboyancy, creativity, and eclectic flowing moves, which terrifies me.

We were trying to dance with our heads instead of our hearts. We were too focused on the learning and the steps and the timing and not enough on the flow and the rhythm and the flare that is so important to dancing. Since then, I've learned many metaphors about how dancing is like therapy and even how counseling theories are like salsa dancing. There are clear and identifiable steps to the salsa (and to theories), but when it all comes together, there is a lot of style, flair, and personality.

Just like dancing, there are many different ways of doing counseling, and these are identified as distinct theories. The major theorists in our field have found a way to make therapy their own. They took foundational principles about how clients change and added their own flair to them, took this away and added that, and created a new theory. But you know what makes each of them unique? They were created by unique people. They found *their* way of doing something very similar to what others were already doing and created their own theory from it. Then, just like that, we have a plethora of counseling theories.

Theories provide us with the structure that is needed, like salsa dancing. We need to learn the steps, the moves, and the directions so we don't trip and fall. Theories provide us with this. Theory provides us with a map or directions for getting from point A to point B with clients. And having these directions is incredibly important to the growth process with clients. As beginners, we really want to have that map, the one that tells us these are the steps you take and then healing will happen. These are the things you can do to prepare for a session, because we all know having a plan makes us feel a lot more grounded and prepared for sessions. But if you've done this work at all yet, you've likely started to learn that the best-laid plan often doesn't even end up being used. We learn that we want to get from point A to point B, and there are a million different roads to take to get there.

Just Sing

My college friend (who actually led me into the field of counseling) was a music major in college. When we were talking about this concept, she shared a story: "I'm reminded of a voice lesson in college when Carolyn [her voice instructor] finally said, 'would you just forget everything I've just told you and just sing?' It was a huge moment of realization for me. I was so stuck on the formality of what I'd been taught that I forgot to just sing!"

While learning the mechanics of our art is incredibly important, it also pulls us away from the heart of this work. The mechanics of integrating theory into our work is important head work, but it pulls us away from the reasons we came into this field. There are reasons we don't just sing, and we'll explore those together in the pages ahead. And as we do, my hope is that my words will give you permission to lessen your grip as you make more space for YOU to come into the room. My hope is that you will begin to rest in the fact that you've learned so much, read so many books, and written so many papers (or will) that provide a solid foundation for you, and now it's time to find your heart in all of these spaces. To invite yourself into the process. To find and be reminded of your *why*. And to remember to *just sing*.

CHAPTER TWO

Ghosts in the Nursery

T here's a video I show in class all the time. I both love and
dread the video. I love the video because of the deep
connection that the students and I have with its contents
and the impact of the message. I dread the video because of the
poignancy of the message and the anguish my heart feels. It's
brutal and breathtaking all at the same time. I give a warning to
my students before I show it. It's heart-wrenching. Students cry.
I cry. It's heart-wrenching because it resonates with us—deeply.
We can identify with it. It makes us *feel*, and feel deeper than we
sometimes care to. We can resonate with the experiences from
different perspectives based on our own experiences.

The video is called the Still Face Experiment[1] that was conducted by Dr. Edward Tronick. In the experiment, a child around one year of age and her mom face one another and interact in playful ways, touching one another with their hands and smiling at each other. At one point, for the purposes of the experiment, the mom turns away from the child, and when she turns back, her face is stoic, stone-like, and apathetic. The child tries to engage with the mom, but the mom remains motionless with a "still face." The child reaches, screeches, and becomes visibly upset that the mom is not responding or engaging with her bids for connection. Soon, the child begins to cry, arch her back, and reach for the mom in a distressed cry. Eventually (which seems like an eternity), the mom reaches for her child, softens, and engages with her facial expressions. Their reengagement is beautiful and touching as the mom meets the child's emotional needs and cries.

Some of us identify with or feel for the mom in the experiment. We can feel her exhaustion, apathy, or confusion about how to help. Sometimes we just want to shut down and disconnect as the needs of others feel too much. Many of us identify with the baby in the experiment. We may be intimately familiar with the blank stares from our own caregivers or partners as we've reached for them. We know, to our core, what it feels like to reach for someone and not be met. We feel the desire to connect with someone and have a desperation to feel comforted and responded to in our pain, in our confusion, and in our sadness. We desire to have someone share in our celebrations and our joy. We deeply desire—or know the long-ago feeling of desire—to be in a relationship with someone.

When we are young, we all have experiences that shape what we believe to be true about relationships. As in the Still Face Experiment, if the responses from our caregivers are consistently rejecting, apathetic, and disconnected, we begin to frame our worth and relationships from those experiences. Often, these experiences with others can also send messages to us about ourselves. The messages speak to the very core of who we are and our inherent worth and value.

Because of those rejections, real or perceived, we translate these statements to "I'm not worthy," "I can't do this," "I'm bad," or "I'm unlovable." And guess what? We hang onto these. Like it or not, these can become permanent tattoos on our hearts that define our worth. We start walking through the world believing "I'm a mistake," "I'm never good enough," "I'm not smart enough," "I'm too fat," "I'm too thin." These messages can become constant second nature and follow us around like ghosts, haunting our relationships, our thoughts, our parenting, our marriage, and our careers.

Ghosts Of Your Past

In the 1970s, a child psychoanalyst named Selma Fraiberg introduced the metaphor of "ghosts in the nursery."2 The idea is that our early relationships with our caregivers impact our own parenting styles. It suggests, similar to the Still Face Experiment, that our early experiences can quite significantly shape our future selves. And when we have negative experiences, these become ghosts that haunt our future reactions to others, our ability to show up, and our self-image. Have you ever said, "I won't do that to my kids when I'm a parent..." and then do that exact thing? Those are impacts from our ghosts, shaping who we become in all aspects of life—and they follow us around for years to come. Fraiberg's research shows that, unfortunately, when children grow up, they can inflict similar experiences or behaviors on their children and others around them.

> Like it or not, these can become permanent tattoos on our hearts that define our worth.

We all have "ghosts in the nursery," whether from the literal nursery, from a previous marriage, from a coach on a soccer field or a gymnastics mat, or from a set of peers in elementary school. We all have experiences from our past that negatively shape what we believe about ourselves. These ghosts don't have to be from our infancy; they can be any experiences that negatively impact the way we move through our days. These ghosts follow us around in all aspects of our lives and into our counseling rooms. While I've worked fairly diligently on silencing these ghosts, sometimes they sneak under the door frames. For me, some of the ghosts from my past include what success looks like, examples of both healthy and unhealthy marriages, perfectionism, pride, and anxiety.

Some of you might be thinking to yourself, "Oh, not me. I had a normal, healthy childhood and great experiences with others. I've got a good career, good friends, and an overall great life with some bumps along the way." I hear you. I see you. And I believe you. I also know that we often don't think we have ghosts that will show up in our work as counselors—and then, POOF! There they are. Or worse, they show up and we don't even realize they're there. And in the counseling room, that's not good for us or our clients.

I had a graduate student who would have disagreed if I had said to him, "We all have ghosts." He would have shared that while he believes others have ghosts in the nursery that follow them into their work as a counselor, his life was pretty amazing overall and he doesn't feel negatively impacted by his prior experiences, and, while open to the possibility that something might come up, he was fairly confident countertransference would not be a struggle for him.

He started the program, wrote amazing papers, and shared thoughtful perspectives in the classroom. But when it came to the role-plays and his client couple didn't quite agree with his attempts to make their marriage healthier, he became slightly irritated—particularly with the wife. When I noticed this with him and invited him to be curious about this with me and shuttle from his head to his heart, I could see tears forming in his eyes. His ghosts were much more recent, related to a past romantic experience, and, as you might guess, he went on to share irritations with his former partner that sounded similar to those shared by his female client.

Some of our ghosts are really obvious. They hover intrusively in our spaces, in our margins, in our homes, and in our heads and hearts. But many other times, our ghosts show up like this example. They hover and sneak and are incredibly intangible as they haunt our minds and hearts, waiting to be tripped over. Most of these ghosts are rooted in interpretations of reality that were formed in previous experiences, from early childhood to the more recent past, and we rely on them (perhaps inappropriately) for guidance. These ghosts tell us who we are, what we can expect from others, and how to respond in any given situation. Our responses and reactions are often built around experiences from our past, whether good or bad, and we move through life making decisions, especially in the counseling room, based on these experiences.

Embrace Your Ghosts

All of these ghosts play a part in our story and create an inner voice or narrative that brings self-doubt and insecurity, whether it be abusive relationships, divorce, trauma, hurts, insecurities, neglect, abandonment, mental illness, or a combination of those. Our experiences and trauma teach us who we can or cannot count on, including our own selves. Our ghosts remind us that we are "screwed up," "broken," and "damaged goods" who need to do our own work. Some of the best therapists I know experience:

Mental health diagnoses
Histories of trauma
Imposter syndrome
Affairs
Dysfunctional families
Doubt in their ability to work in this field
Addiction
Divorce
Insecurity

If you read this list and can identify with one or two or six of these experiences, you are not alone. Fellow human, I see you and I'm with you. Me too. I've lived a storied life, and I know many of you have, too. You've experienced pain and suffering, loneliness and abuse, neglect and addiction. Who or what are your ghosts? Do you know them, or some of them? I know many of mine, and some are walled up pretty tight from others—and even myself sometimes. I like to pretend that if I keep them sealed off and hidden, I'm protected from them. But that's not the truth at all. You see, our ghosts can permeate walls. They go straight through, their transparency not impacted at all by barriers, bricks, or doors. Despite how strong we think our walls are in keeping the ghosts out, they come straight through, like water through a bucket with a hole in it.

If I'm being honest, it's scary for me to share my own ghosts with you because many of my ghosts are still hovering. They still impact me. Most of them impact me less than they used to because I've gotten to know them. It's almost as if I can now see them hovering, and I mostly choose not to let them impact my work. But they're still in my life, and I love many of them. I don't share these stories publicly to protect them.

But I want you to know, friend, that they're there, dancing around even as I write these words—almost snickering at me because I just admitted they are still there. And when they snicker, I feel small. I feel insignificant. I feel my body warm and tears form in my eyes. The tears come because I both love and hate the ghosts, and that feels heavy and overwhelming. And I bet you have many of those, too. And guess what? That doesn't mean you can't do this work. Let me say that again: it doesn't mean you can't do this work. It means I'm in good company with you and you with me. It means we're human and have lived storied lives. And it means we have work to do, our own work of naming these ghosts and getting familiar with them. My ghosts of anxiety, which hang around pretty obviously, stem from a number of experiences in my long ago and more recent past.

They've been around so long I think the anxiety ghosts had baby anxiety ghosts, and they hang around, too.

> And, when we work through our ghosts, we can become angels for others in their grief and trauma.

Sometimes my ghosts show up in the words I speak to my young daughter, and I see evidence of generational trauma that I know each generation just tries to do a little bit better. And sometimes I cry alone because the ghosts feel so powerful and I want to keep them to myself. I want to keep my grief and regret and shame to myself about failing (again) to battle the ghosts. Sometimes my angel husband sees evidence of these ghosts and blankets me with understanding and love. Guess what? We have angels in the nursery as well. I'll unpack this more in future chapters, but we have angels that battle the ghosts. These angels often come in secure attachment and unconditional love. And I'm thankful for that. And, when we work through our ghosts, we can become angels for others in their grief and trauma. That's the work of a counselor. But before we can become angels for others in their healing journeys, we must face our ghosts. Hard stop. *You, dear friend, must face your own ghosts.*

Name Your Ghosts

Take a moment to name your ghosts in the margin, in your head, in a journal, wherever you want to acknowledge your awareness. Right now, shuttle from your head to your heart and back to your head and explore who and what your ghosts are—the ones you think will impact your work as a counselor and the ones you think won't sneak into that space at all. Name them. There's a phrase coined by psychiatrist Dan Siegel where he suggests we "name it to tame it"[3] as a technique to notice and label emotions, which can reduce stress and anxiety in the brain and body. This can apply here to our ghosts as well. Just start naming, for yourself and your own work, what and who these ghosts might be that will show up in the counseling room as you work with others. There is great, important work in naming these ghosts.

Do you drink too much after a long day? Does your depression become crippling and keep you hiding under the bed sheets? Does your anger show up in how you treat others? Does your anger stay at bay during the work day and come out to the people you love the most once you're at home? Does your relationship with food and/or your body cause you to hide these fears? Does your relationship with a man from your past make you dread working with men? Does your previous experience with God or God-followers make you avoid Christians at all costs?

How's that list of ghosts coming along? Did I just add to your list? Is your list becoming long? Mine too. That list comes from personal struggles and struggles others have shared with me about their ghosts. Sometimes, naming these ghosts can be overwhelming and scary. It's incredibly normal to be scared and apprehensive to acknowledge your ghosts and begin the process of silencing them.

You are allowed to be scared. You are allowed to struggle and feel lost. You are allowed to feel (or be!) behind the learning curve of others. You are allowed to have your own therapist to do this work. You are allowed to feel like maybe you can't do this. You are allowed to be a learner. You are allowed to have ghosts and be scared to discover just how many or how big or how haunting they are. I know you're scared to share them with others. I know you're thinking, "They don't know just how broken I am," and you want to keep it that way because if they do, they will tell you not to do this work. Some of our ghosts actually tell us *not* to seek help or listen to our bodies or trust others, and the fear of doing the work is the actual ghost itself.

Whether we like it or not, or are aware of it or not, we all have ghosts. Or, as I sometimes like to say in class to normalize this experience, "We all have sh$#." And it's true; we do. Even the tenured professor at the front of the room with over twenty years of clinical experience...perhaps *especially* the tenured professor at the front of the room with over twenty years of clinical experience. We all have ghosts, and we all have work to be done to identify these ghosts.

As you read in the last chapter, we all come to this work of being a counselor for a reason. For many of us, those reasons are because of our own scars, our own pain, and our deep desire to help others through the pain, either in the beautiful and tender ways that others served us or in ways that others didn't meet our basic needs. Sometimes this baggage we carry around haunts us like the ghosts in the nursery. It follows us into our work and causes us to be blind-sided, cause harm to others (clients and otherwise), and stay in the pain space.

Other times, if we do our own work, our previous baggage can become our most important tool. It can become our most significant opportunity to connect with others in ways other therapists cannot. Reader, your experiences of ghosts or brokenness can be the most important and strongest way you connect and empathize with others. Your brokenness can be your strength.

> For most students, the biggest roadblock to becoming a counselor is not the book learning but the emotional courage to face our inner ghosts and unravel the layers to finding our true selves.

Facing, naming, and taming our ghosts can be scary. Often, when we are open, honest, and raw, it bites us in the butt, and we regret ever opening our mouth. Throughout my years as a professor and supervisor, I have had many students who wanted to become counselors while keeping these walls up and trying to protect their inner worlds. They tried to stay in the head space in the hope of avoiding their own feelings, emotions, and ghosts. As much as you think your professors can't see them, we can (at least, those of us who are looking can). I can see, almost feel, the fear and the sadness because I can sense the pain beneath your need for disconnection. These attempts to intellectualize your way through becoming a counselor prevent personal growth and the development of your therapeutic self and abilities. For most students, the biggest roadblock to becoming a counselor is not the book learning but the emotional courage to face our inner ghosts and unravel the layers to finding our true selves.

There may be a thousand reasons to stay in your pain, unwilling or unable to let go. And there are hundreds of amazing books written about this trauma and ways to begin that work. You can stop there if you want to. But whole only comes after broken. Healing only comes after wounds. If you haven't started, it's time to do your own work. Your future clients are worth it. *You are worth it.*

My great invitation is that we discover we can have both ghosts and angels hovering while making mistakes or working through our yuck. You can be committed to learning and grow-ing rather than be a counselor who arrives in a state of perfection and never makes mistakes.

I'm working with an intern who has ghosts from her past related to what being in a healthy, committed relationship looks like. She knows this about herself and still wants to be a compe-tent marriage counselor. But she doesn't actually know what a healthy marriage looks like. So, while her ghosts float around re-minding her of mistakes and insecurities, she pushes them away by seeking healthy marriage mentors. She asks her professors for examples she can sink into learning about. In her role-plays, she seeks out areas where she needs the work rather than something easier. She engages in personal and professional conversations about how she will battle these ghosts while also learning about the angels that can be in this space.

Other new counselors choose not to do the work that is required until it's right in their face and we find ourselves being critical or completely withdrawn or angry or disassociated. And even then, it's scary to face the reality of how our ghosts showed up in those moments. Unfortunately, our brains are set up for survival and defense; thus, we remember painful events much more fluidly than the pleasant ones. We remember the A- we got in grad school rather than the several A's we earned. We remember the dog bite more than the beautiful sunset. And we know this is true. If you get five compliments on your counseling role-plays and one piece of criticism, what's the one piece you remember the most? The criticism! Psychologist Rick Hanson coined the phrase, "The brain is Velcro for negative experienc-es, but Teflon for positive ones."4 Our ghosts tend to be far more present than our angels are. This is why we need to do the work to understand our ghosts, to name them, tame them, and rearrange the landscape of what our brains and our hearts hang onto. This is incredibly important work.

> The ghosts you're not facing will follow you into the therapy room.

I am not minimizing the presence of our ghosts or saying they are easy to kick out of our hearts. As a trauma therapist, I've seen great pain, and I know that progress is slow and steady. I know this, and I honor this. My hope is that you begin the work and just keep swimming. Just keep fighting for you. We need to battle our ghosts because when we don't, they become a liability. The feelings left unmonitored will not just go away. They won't fly out the door and leave to haunt someone else. They won't get bored and pack up. These ghosts find a way to linger and multiply. When we don't fight against these ghosts, we can't heal others. How can we ask our clients to do the work that we aren't willing to do ourselves? The ghosts you're not facing will follow you into the therapy room.

Face Your Ghosts

There's a children's book I read out loud to my students sometimes. It's fun to see how grown adults get so excited for class story time. The book is called *Going on a Bear Hunt*[5] and it tells the story of a family who goes on a bear hunt to look for bears (I'm not sure why). But the metaphor is powerful, so as I share the story, think about what these obstacles they encounter represent for you. It starts by showing pictures of the family and tells the story:

"We're going on a bear hunt
We're going to catch a big one

What a beautiful day,
we're not scared."

Then, the family encounters the first obstacle of grass, and they say:

"Uh oh! Long wavy grass
We can't go over it
We can't go under it
We've got to go through it."

Then, the reader can make sounds of grass and movement of grass with their hands. This happens five times, starting with the first phrase, "We're going on a bear hunt...we're not scared..." followed by obstacles which get more intense the further along they get. The family encounters a river—a deep, cold river—then thick, oozy mud. Then they encounter a big, dark forest, and they can't go over it, they can't go under it, they've got to go through it. Then a swirling whirling snowstorm which they, you guessed it, go through.

Finally, they encounter a "narrow, gloomy cave," and they decide to go through that as well. At the back of the cave, they discover the bear and run away from the bear back to their safe home. The message in this book is that whatever we encounter in life, in our counseling room with our own ghosts, we can't go over the obstacles, and we can't go under them—we have to go through them. And it helps to have friends with you, battling all the ghosts along the way, together.

The process of going through our obstacles, facing our ghosts, and doing our own work is hard yet *crucial* work. You can't skip this step. You can't go around it or over it or under it.

You will get activated by clients. You will get triggered. It's just a matter of when and how much. You have to go through it. Begin working on these ghosts by inviting others to help you. Many of us find the best way to do that is through our own therapy. Yes, therapists need therapy. This is ongoing, lifelong work—not just a quick fix of our past, but a constant process of discovering and rediscovering and tripping and stumbling along the way. This work is done in relationship with our own therapists, our supervisors, and in consultation with other counselors who can help us see these blind spots so we can lessen their impact on others we work with in our role as counselors.

Thankfully, due to important work in neuroplasticity and trauma,[6] we now know that our brains can change. These permanent tattoos from our past can be less permanent, and our most deeply rooted habits and behaviors can be deconditioned. By doing our own work, we can silence our ghosts. This is celebration-worthy. It shows that our work as counselors *works* and that we can help change the trajectory of pain and suffering. Over time, our ghosts and our work to silence our ghosts help make us compassionate, empathic providers. With corrective emotional experiences, we can invite our ghosts to go.

When we invite our ghosts to go, we become more open to healing, health, and using our brokenness to hold the pain and suffering of others. Our brokenness can serve a purpose. In Japan, broken objects are sometimes repaired with gold. The process, called Kintsugi (golden joinery), is an art used to repair broken pottery. The broken pieces of pottery are put back together using gold to fill in the broken pieces and edges and return it to its original shape, with gold highlighting the cracks and flaws. The flaw is seen as a unique piece of the object's history, which adds to its beauty.

The ancient art form so beautifully reflects life, brokenness, and healing. Even in the midst of brokenness, beauty can be found, and what was once broken can be mended into something that is stronger than its original form. The pottery can become more beautiful after being broken. I think we are like this, too, you and me, reader.

My brokenness and your brokenness is what makes us unique and beautiful and strong. Our ghosts, things we can think are areas of weakness, can actually be our superpower. There is purpose in our scars, in our brokenness. If we spend the time healing them and putting the broken art back together, this broken piece of art can be one that holds others. That holds pain. That holds suffering. Our brokenness, our ghosts, can become a point of connection and hope for others. There is purpose in your scars, but you must first do the work. You must do your work. You are worth it.

CHAPTER THREE

"What the Hell am I Doing Here?"

Any second now, one of my professors or supervisors is going to pull me into their office and have a "heart-to-heart" conversation with me. I know how this conversation goes; I've already had it at least forty times in my head. It's the conversation where they give me a compliment sandwich—they tell me something positive and encouraging about my "eagerness" or my "dedication to learning" or something they try to make sound positive that I don't even hear because I know the next part is coming. Then, they share all the bad news in the middle and sandwich it with another compliment to try to make the bad not feel so bad. In that middle section of the sandwich, they tell me things like "not ready" and "do more of my own work" or "consider other professions." It's where they say I don't have what it takes to do the work of a counselor, and they expose me as the fraud that I am. Where they tell me:

I'm not good enough
I'm not cut out for this
I'm not qualified enough
I'm too damaged
I'm too young/old/sensitive/assertive

This is where the fears of my heart come to life in the words of someone else to me. If I let that sink in, into the deep spaces

I hide from most people, and really feel this fear of someone exposing me as a fraud, it's terrifying. Imposter syndrome, by nature, only shows up when we really care deeply about something and are trying so desperately to be good at it and demonstrate to others that we are good enough at it. We want our supervisors, clients, colleagues, and professors to know that we can figure it out. That we have what it takes. That we are good enough in our actions and in our hearts.

I have a clear and vivid memory of my very first client, over twenty years ago. I wish I didn't remember, and I bet he does, too. I was in my counseling master's program, and we were doing our practicum, our first opportunity to sit with real clients with real problems. The clients were from the university undergraduate program. I sat and watched each of my fellow classmates meet with these college students through a one-way mirror. The clients were coming with roommate problems, were unsure which degree to major in, and had fears about disappointing their parents. Us counselors were about three-fourths of the way through our counseling degree program. We were nervous, and our professor reassured us that our clients were more nervous than we were and told us to just "relax into the space."

I kept running those two comments through my head, "they are more nervous than me" and "relax into the space." I remember thinking to myself, "If they are more nervous than I am, this doesn't bode well for me because I am a WRECK of nerves." The client came in and shook my hand, and I pulled away and had to wipe the sweat from his handshake that left near puddles in my palm. Believe it or not, he *was* more nervous than me.

I had a prepared list of questions at the ready, and had

memorized the order, the pace, and the inflection, and I felt ready. I finally got to the magic question that jumps us into rapport-building and problem-solving and asked, "What brings you in today?" This kind, nervous, young human proceeded to share, without coming up for air, his significantly disruptive obsessive-compulsive behaviors, his deep fears around these compulsions disrupting his career aspirations, and the rather extensive childhood trauma that he believed his OCD stemmed from.

He talked for about 15 minutes straight, baring his heart, history, vulnerabilities, and insecurities. And then he stopped. Completely. And looked at me. With longing eyes communicating, "Please tell me I'm okay! Tell me I'm not too much for you! Tell me we're gonna figure this out together." Guess what I said. I said nothing. Zip. Zilch. Nada! I froze. I remember trying to coax myself to say something. "Ask a question!" I coaxed myself. "Use validation," I continued silently to myself. Say something, *anything*...where was the basic empathy statement? Where were the summarizing skills?

I thought to myself...
Wait, is this for real?
This isn't for real; this is my nightmare...just SPEAK, MICHELLE.
Someone, please come in here and *help me*!
Hello? Is anyone coming? This dear human needs an ACTUAL THERAPIST HERE!

Ummmm....is nobody stepping in? You mean it's just me and him? For an hour? What am I supposed to do? What am I supposed to say? How can confused and overwhelmed me help him with these real problems?

Talk about feeling out of my element. I shed a lot of tears following that session. That was my first ever session, and I had bombed it. Failed miserably. Failed the client, failed myself, and confirmed to the whole world that I was completely useless and an utter failure as a therapist. I felt immense shame, embarrassment, and doubt. I wanted to hide. As I reflect on the story here in these words, I can feel my heart racing and my body preparing me for tears. I still feel shame, 20 years later, that I couldn't be with this human in the ways he so desperately needed and deserved. And it was recorded, too, so I had the privilege of watching the video and critiquing myself through an assigned paper. How on earth do you write an eight-page paper that simply says, "I did everything wrong."

Am I Really Good Enough?

After that session, and many other sessions that were a somewhat less dramatic version (the client shared and I felt inadequate in my response or presence), I've learned that it's really common to feel these paralyzing fears. It's common to feel that we aren't doing enough in our work with clients, and it's common for these fears to make us freeze or fumble or both.

For many of us, starting to be a counselor feels a lot like putting on a counselor suit and playing the role until it feels like our own. But until that time, we feel like big huge imposters. Imposter syndrome is the constant nagging voice that says, "Who am I to provide therapy?" or "Am I really qualified to counsel others?" or even "Why should clients listen to *me*?" The ghosts from our past show up in all kinds of places, and they often look like imposter syndrome, too. We feel like we've fooled people

into believing we have what it takes to do this work, and one of
these days, we're going to get discovered.

> For many of us, starting to be a counselor feels a lot
> like putting on a counselor suit and playing the role
> until it feels like our own. But until that time, we feel
> like big fat imposters.

Imposter syndrome is when we dwell in heaps of self-doubt
and don't trust our experience and training. Even when others
might believe in us and our abilities, imposter syndrome holds
us hostage to the belief that we don't have what it takes. It makes
us feel, despite all our knowledge to the contrary, that others are
better equipped, that they innately have more skills or natural
abilities than we do.

So you feel like you have to hide. You fear being discovered. You fear you don't really know what you thought you did.
You try to hide your belief that you're not enough. You wonder
why you have to work so hard at what comes so easily for everyone else.

You feel lost
Alone
Overwhelmed
Stuck
Stupid

As I pondered what to write about in a chapter on imposter
syndrome, honestly, part of me just wanted to fill this entire
chapter with phrases I've heard from counselors and counselors
in training over the years. I want you to hear all the things that so
many of us say about ourselves and our journey to becoming a
counselor. I desperately want you to feel that you are not alone.

These spaces where you doubt yourself matter to me, for you. In these spaces where you feel like quitting, I want you to feel someone there as your cheerleader. When these voices tell you you'll never be good enough, I want you to open to these pages and read that it's okay to have doubts, it's okay to have ghosts, it's okay to have fears that you're not cut out for this. But in these pages, I want the messages and words to hug you, and I want you to hear them say, "Me too, dear friend. I'm scared, too. I'm scared when I feel so alone and these messages are so loud. Me, too, dear friend—when these fears of self-doubt fill my heart so loudly that I can't even scare them away. Me, too, dear friend. I feel fear, self-doubt, comparison, and brokenness."

Am I Alone In This?

All those people you compare yourself to (your fellow class-mates, your colleagues, clinicians who are licensed, your professors), those people who seem confident also feel self-doubt and insecurity. They, too, say things like, "I'm not good enough for this," and "Someone is going to find out I don't know what I'm doing and kick me out." Everyone has good ways of hiding their fears and insecurities. Just because we don't see people strug-gling does not mean they aren't. We are all waiting for someone to discover that we don't really know what we are doing.

> When these voices tell you you'll never be good enough, I want you to open to these pages and read that it's okay to have doubts, it's okay to have ghosts, it's okay to have fear that you're not cut out for this.

I reached out and asked counselors to share their imposter syndrome messages, and I want you to hear them. I want you to read the experiences of people just like you. I want you to circle them, underline them, and highlight them. I want you to read the self-doubt, fear, comparison, and messages that people shared with you through me. I want you to read these and know:

You are not alone
You are not more broken than anyone else
These messages of self-doubt are powerful
They are relentless

I want you to know when you feel like you have to hide in fear of being discovered, that it doesn't come easy for anyone. You are not the only one who is lost, overwhelmed, and stuck.

These aren't phrases I made up; these are words that people close to me entrusted to me and to you, sweet human, to help you feel that you are journeying with others just like you. These are real people with real worries about showing up to do this work who have fears that nag at them and tell them to run away. These are people I love, and I feel honored to share their stories and experiences of imposter syndrome:

"Imposter syndrome hits hardest when my inner critic asks, 'What makes you think you can help others?' My inner critic says things like, 'You don't even have your own life figured out.'"

"Feeling like a fraud [...] These people pay me to help fix their problems, but I am just going with it and journeying with them but not actually helping them."

"What the heck am I doing here? What do I know? Why did I ever think I could help anybody? I feel like a little girl dressed up in her mommy's clothes, pretending to be "big" and not kidding anybody. I want to run away and hide."

"Feeling that I don't have what it takes. That I'm not talented enough, smart enough, strong enough, sensitive enough, stable enough, experienced enough… to be a counselor."

"Imposter syndrome is my baseline. It's a loud voice to try to ignore. It yells that I am too young, too unqualified, too uneducated, too female, too millennial to have the privilege and luck I have, especially in my professional achievements. [...] I don't feel I deserve to (or even should) be at the tables I hold a seat at."

"Imposter syndrome feels like I am a fraud and a con, and at any minute, people will find out just how big of a dummy I am. It looks like comparison of how other clinicians and their careers differ from my own. It shows up in second-guessing every choice I make in treatment planning, paralysis on what word to use in a note, so then I get stuck on a note for hours that should only take me 10 minutes to write."

If you feel these deeply, or parts of these, you are in good company. You are not alone. What would you add to this list? How does imposter syndrome show up that is unique to you? Everyone feels like an imposter sometimes. It's true, everyone! Your professor? Imposter. Your boss? Imposter. Your dad? Imposter. Your dentist? Imposter. Your colleague who is brilliant/astute/has a niche? Yup! Imposter. It's normal to feel like you're the only one who feels like a fraud, especially when there are constant messages that you are not smart enough, successful enough, eclectic enough, theoretically grounded enough, and your best grad school buddy receives more awards/internships/assistantships/scholarships than you.

Today, as I write, this is my imposter voice. It says, "Ha! See, I told you you suck. These words suck. These sentences don't make sense; this doesn't flow. You should quit and go back to what you were doing before. You don't belong here; leave this to people who are good at it. Stop while you're ahead before you make a fool out of yourself, before you pour even more time and energy and money into this. Stop before you embarrass yourself and your family."

And sometimes I really do want to stop, quit, run away, and stick my head in the sand, and I bet you do, too. Anyone who has ever done something new that they really care deeply about has felt like an imposter. One of my writing mentors, a beautifully talented human, Emily P. Freeman, wrote, "I talk to myself with my critical hat on. It is black and has a feather, and critical Emily knows everything. She knows why I am an idiot. She's memorized my weaknesses and recites them at all the worst times. She makes a little rhyme and puts them in a song, and that nasty tune weaves its sticky melody through every corner of hope in my heart."[1] Our ghosts are happy to sing these melodies to us as we move through this process of becoming and being a counselor.

What If I Don't Jump?

These ghosts of imposter syndrome show up in all aspects of our lives. And when they do, they can be sneaky and transfer fears from one area to fears in another area of our lives. A few years ago, I went to an aerial adventure park with a few fearless friends. We were pumped up, ready to conquer the course and come back and report to our children how fearless and brave we were in hopes they would grow into our paths of courage as they adventure through life.

This adventure park has several obstacle courses set high in the trees. Each course has a sequence of challenging obstacles between trees that include Tarzan swings, balance beams, ladders, wobbly bridges, tight ropes, and zip lines, with increasing difficulty the further you go. Of course, I was harnessed in, but who really believes in our security blankets? Most of us do not; we desperately want to not need them and be successful on our own without needing help.

I bet you think you know where this is going: I fell and was caught by my harness, and it was a beautiful and inspiring lesson in trust. Nope. Not it. We were high in the trees and on the second to the last and hardest obstacle. The obstacle was to jump from one small platform to another small platform, leaping the five feet between the two. Two friends went ahead of me, braving the ravenous jump with apparent ease and little discomfort.

It was my turn, and I had one friend behind me. My mind was playing violent tricks on me, telling me things that weren't true. That I would fall to a violent death. Or that I would jump and not make it and whack my head on the platform, cracking it wide open. The images running through my head were colorful and vivid. And the messages...oh, the messages... "You'll get hurt. You can't do this. You're only just over five feet yourself. Your other friends are much taller than you. You're an embarrassment. You're holding everyone up. Everyone else is doing it. You're a failure. Your daughter is going to be disappointed." That last one was a big one for me. "Your daughter is going to be disappointed. She won't be proud of you. She won't love you as much as she did before. You are a huge disappointment to her." It still brings me to tears as I write it.

You know what happened? I didn't jump. My mind was too

strong (weak?) to let me jump. The self-doubt was fierce. I felt like an imposter who had just left my young daughter at home, basically telling her I was going out to conquer all my fears and be her superwoman and role model. I was ashamed, and everything I had told my daughter was bullcrap. About being a strong woman. About being able to conquer our fears. About being able to do things that scare us. About trying new things. And the best (worst) part? There was no ladder down, nope. The *rescue squad* had to come up the tree and harness, strap, buckle, backpack me onto them, and carry me down like a baby monkey on their back. This grown-ass woman let her fears prevent her from moving forward.

The message here isn't about facing our fears, although that could be relevant as well. The message here is that our self-doubt is powerful. The self-doubt that creeps in high in the trees or in other activities, sports, or hobbies we do can show up in the counseling room, too. Those doubts that said, "You can't do this," and "You're an embarrassment," and "Everyone else is doing it," don't just show up in the treetops; they show up for me in the counseling room. And those quotes about imposter syndrome shared by the brave others are from ghosts, and those ghosts don't discern where they show up—they show up everywhere. And chipping away at it is a slow process.

The self-doubt, fear, and imposter syndrome come from a lot of different places. Most of the time, these messages come from our ghosts and the stories they've been telling us for years, sometimes decades. Or, for me, the ghosts I had been ignoring by just doing the next thing, earning the next degree, getting the next award. In some areas of my life, success came easy for me, so I did more of that and less of the things that made me feel insecure, less than, and imperfect. I thought I could outrun my self-doubt. It was a horrible lie. It's still a horrible lie I tell myself sometimes.

What's Underneath?

The tricky thing is, imposter syndrome is a cover. It hides deeper, more painful, and true underlying emotions that are much more difficult for us to identify and feel, for good reasons. Emotionally focused therapy,[2] founded by Sue Johnson, introduces the idea of primary and secondary emotions. This theory suggests that we all have secondary emotions that protect our deeper, more vulnerable primary emotions. For example, my expressed frustration or annoyance prevents me from sinking into my feelings of loneliness or abandonment, my primary emotions. In the case of imposter syndrome, feeling like an imposter is a secondary emotion that hides our more vulnerable, sensitive, sometimes hidden primary emotion. Often, when we feel like an imposter, it's important to identify the more hidden primary emotion. While hanging in the trees, I felt fear, like a big, fake, brave mom—but the underlying primary emotions were embarrassment, frailty, fallibility, and failure. My imperfection would be on display as I told my daughter I didn't complete the course. And sitting in those emotions was where the real, raw work was needed.

Pushing back the fear or the imposter syndrome is a lifelong process. No matter how brave we get, it's so easy to pick up those messages and carry them with us. It's comfortable. We know all the words, we know the actions, and it's an easy space to settle back into. Moving away from the fear that we have nothing to offer takes intentional effort, and you are worth that effort. The old parts of us that are the most difficult to shed are the core beliefs that something is wrong with us, that we are deficient, flawed, or worthless. However, in order to remove this old belief system and self-doubt, we must continue to grow. When we continue to grow, we shed the old skin that no longer fits us.

> Moving away from the fear that we have nothing to offer takes intentional effort, and you are worth that effort.

This process of shedding our skin for future growth is reflected in nature and is called ecdysis, the process snakes go through when they shed their skin. Snakes shed their skin because it no longer fits or because it's old or worn out—essentially, they begin to outgrow it. For a snake to shed its skin, the snake must rub against something abrasive, like a rock, or like our growth edges, insecurities, and imposter syndrome. The rubbing against causes a tear, which the snake can use to start the process of shedding. Interestingly, while shedding the skin mostly serves as a part of a snake's growing process, it also helps remove parasites that can harm the snake. Nature has a built-in shedding system to rid ourselves of parasites and dead skin as we grow. We, too, must shed our layers that hold us back, over and over again, just like a snake. Snakes shed their skin four to twelve times a year. Think of all the parasites we might be carrying around with us when we don't go through that shedding process.

Under the dead skin shed by a snake is new skin. We, too, have new skin. At the end of a course that I teach, I ask the students to engage in a creative exercise. I encourage them to think about the ways they've grown and the ways that they can see themselves being a counselor differently than at the beginning of the class. I ask them to think about how they've seen themselves showing up, growing, and recognizing what this new skin might look like. I draw a picture on the board of a tree with leaves, blooms, buds, and new growth. The green leaves on the tree represent the growth that happens every time we sit with clients or learn something new about life, counseling, or ourselves. We sit in silence, and I ask them to finish the sentence, "I AM...." that is written above the blooming tree. Then, one at a time, they share their word or phrase that completes the sentence. I write them on the board on the growth of the tree. There's no discussion, no explanations or justifications or minimizations. We simply share, write, and reflect together on the growing list on the growing tree.

They write: I am...creative, introspective, accepting, present, brave, authentic, uncomfortable, strong, validating, a layer, trusting, imperfect, meant to be here, letting go, growing.

Spend a moment here, right now, and fill in the blank on the growth of this tree. How are you growing, reader?

I am _____

Do it a few more times. Claim the new skin that is underneath when you shed your doubts and imposter syndrome. Maybe it's not fresh and clean and new every single day. Maybe we immediately slink through the mud and get dirty and lost in the process again, and that's okay. Shedding skin is a process. It takes snakes one to two weeks, and they're tiny little creatures. What is your "I am" statement? Own those words.

I am a beginner. I am imperfect. I am trying. I am authentic. I am strong. I am brave. I am safe. I am growing. I am myself. I am uncomfortable. I am letting go. I am meant to be here. I am a counselor.

This is growth, reader. This is the start of knowing the areas where you are growing and learning and moving from the burden of imposter syndrome to the becoming parts of you.

As I drove up to the house after my tree-to-tree adventure with tears of embarrassment and failure running down my face, my daughter came bounding out of the house, arms outstretched, eager to hear all the details of my heroic bravery in the tall Oregon treetops. The first words out of my lips were that I failed and didn't do the big scary jump at the end.

Through tears, I bent down to her outside my house and told her that sometimes being brave doesn't mean jumping all the time. It was the best I could do to reframe the failure that I was. She hugged me tight around my neck and asked how many I *had* done. The answer was "countless." I had jumped and balanced and crossed and swung across, over and under countless other adventures that day. And she wanted to hear about those. She wanted to know how high and how scary and how tippy and how adventurous *those* were. She wanted to hear about my "I am" statements of courage and growth and not about my "I failed" experiences.

The treetops in that Oregon forest provided an opportunity to dwell on my failures and insecurities and feelings of being an imposter, or to show growth and adventure and all the other aspects of how I showed up that brave, adventurous afternoon. Reader, I invite you to fill up the branches of the tree with words that highlight your adventures of growth and learning and becoming.

PART TWO

Becoming

*"There is no place so awake and alive
as the edge of becoming."*

Sue Monk Kidd [1]

CHAPTER FOUR

Lean into Love

A few years ago, I was preparing a lecture for a counseling internship course where students are in the field meeting with clients and building caseloads, rapport, and therapeutic trust. I wanted to talk in class about the concept of love and how it relates to our work as a counselor. I opened an internet browser and searched for "love and the counseling relationship," hoping it would provide a good layer to the foundational bullet points I had already prepared. This search brought up a bit more than I expected—some relevant, some off-topic, and some concerning, yet realistic, aspects of love in a therapeutic relationship. My results looked a bit like this:

- The Five Love Languages[1]
  (while a good book and tool, not exactly what I was asking for)
- When it's okay to have sex with a client
  (umm…never??)
- Love is Blind[2]
  (a television show that is, how do I say, not the same love that I'm referring to here)
- A whole list of lovely counseling agencies with "love" in the name
  (how lovely)

- Are you in love with your therapist?
  (okay, not exactly what I meant...)
- Why counselors make poor lovers
  (oh boy...)

I was both horrified and, in some ways, not at all surprised. I found nothing helpful that talked about the ways therapists navigate the feeling of (non-erotic) love and admiration in counseling, but found cautions, permissions, and ethical dilemmas abound, and even some suggestions for skirting ethical codes and guidelines to engage in such relationships.

Love is a forbidden word in the context of this work as a counselor. Intimacy is the same, yet that's the very core of the work we do. We create incredibly intimate relationships with people who disclose things to us about their lives that they often do not share with anyone else and have never considered sharing with others. Yet when we lean into our therapeutic relationships, intimacy is developed. But instead of developing love and intimacy with clients, we use other words that feel safer and more disconnected, like alliance, compassion, empathy, and unconditional positive regard to describe the relationship and the feelings that develop within the therapeutic relationship. While these are good descriptions of our work as well, we don't talk about the presence of love in the counseling process. And love in counseling is a beautiful and reparative experience. Maybe even the *most* reparative experience.

Over the years as a professor, I've asked students to co-create a "theme" for the year in their small internship cohort of ten students. Sometimes these themes are phrases like, "You are enough" or "I want to see you be brave," and we spend the year integrating the theme into our reflections and applications to the work of a counselor.

One year, students chose the fruits of the spirit as the theme, as outlined in the Bible in the book of Galatians. While only some of the students identified as Christian, the group decided the "fruits" outlined could be applied to both Christian and secular counselors alike. Each week, we would unpack one of the nine fruits: joy, peace, patience, love, kindness, goodness, faithfulness, gentleness, and self-control.[3] One of those fruits, or counselor characteristics, is love—an often taboo topic when discussing the relationship between client and therapist. When the week of "love" came around and it was time to unpack this in the counseling space, the students looked at each other confused, trepidatious, almost as if to figure out if this was a trap. I invited them to reflect on how love was a part of the work of a counselor. Their reflections included:

"Can we even talk about love in our profession?"
"Aren't there too many red flags for this?"
"Is the ethics board listening to this conversation?"
"Nope, nope, NOPE."
"This is way too complex for my brain today."
"I have clients I like, love, and can't stand—is that okay? Did I share that out loud?"

Even when invited into a conversation, counselors in training didn't want to engage in it. It felt like there were too many landmines to navigate the conversation. And yet, when encouraged to do so, we were able to talk about the fears, the struggles, the pains, the learning opportunities, and the beauty that can emerge when we share our discomfort and fears. We began exploring that there might be a place for love in counseling. And maybe there always had been; we just haven't called it that. Love has been a part of the experience of counseling all along, just blanketed in other words.

> We don't talk about the presence of love in the counseling process. And love in counseling is a beautiful and reparative experience. Maybe even the *most* reparative experience.

Is The Ethics Board Listening?

The truth is, there are some very valid and very concerning aspects that are worth caution signs and disclaimer warnings. The web search captured some of these landmines. The purpose of this book or this chapter is not to teach you about all of the things to avoid or about the ethics of healthy therapeutic relationships, though it is worth highlighting here with an abundance of caution as we talk about love and counseling.

I am not talking about having sex with your clients. I am not talking about sharing your own experiences of love with your client through self-disclosure. I am not talking about leaning into countertransference or your clients fulfilling your unmet needs for love. I am not talking about telling your clients you love them. These and a million others are important ethical guidelines that should be honored and recognized, and their behaviors should be cautioned against.

If you are challenged by any of these, I invite you to reach out to a professor, a colleague, or a supervisor to help dissect these in the ways that are needed for your head and your heart.

Asking questions and seeking consultation is always wise, and I affirm you for doing so whenever you feel lost or confused about anything, but especially about love in the context of counseling. This part of the minefield is avoidable. Do not enter that minefield. Heed the warnings, caution signs, and disclaimers.

Is There A Place For Love?

Love is far more than these warnings and caution signs. We all have many different love relationships in our lives: we love our partners (if we have them), our children, siblings, parents, friends, and neighbors. And it's all love, but it's all different love. When I went to college, I loved my roommates and college friends, and we said "I love you" to each other. I was in a not-so-serious relationship with a boy friend (not yet a boyfriend), and I shared with him that I loved him. I meant it in a non-romantic way, but he and I did not have the same framework around the different messages that "love" could mean (he didn't say "I love you" back). I struggled to understand why he couldn't separate "I love you as a beautiful human" from "I want to marry you, have your babies, and be with you for the rest of our lives."

But love is different between people, and for different reasons. I do not love my husband the same way I love my friends or my daughter. I love my parents differently than my husband's parents. While all love, it's different in how we describe it and different in how it is expressed and felt. Different cultures and diverse relationships view love differently and uniquely as well. How I love my clients is a unique love that is different from how I love others in my life.

Love in the therapeutic relationship is not wrong. Love in the therapeutic relationship can be healing, transformative, and fulfilling. Sure, it can also be misunderstood, confusing, and difficult to express. But the version of love in counseling that I'm talking about here is not holding hands and gazing lovingly into each other's eyes. It's walking alongside clients as they process their trauma, experiences, and losses. It's holding people accountable for their work in becoming healthier. It's encouraging clients to learn healthy ways of getting their needs met in the world.

Love is creating safe spaces for people to unpack their stories, struggle with their relationships and boundaries, and be honest, raw, and vulnerable. Love is listening with the ear of our heart. Love is in the counseling I did last week with a man yearning for connection. It is sharing a space with him, a hurting man who can count on one hand the number of times he's ever cried. Love is heartfelt silence as he cries into his hands, unpacking the ghosts from his past that continue to haunt him today. It is telling him he's brave when he shares he's embarrassed by his tears. It is him believing me when I tell him he's doing beautiful work, even when it's scary and it doesn't feel beautiful.

Love is feeling both professionally and personally impacted by his tears and his trust and feeling my own tears gathering at my bottom eyelids. Love is carrying him in my heart throughout the rest of the day. And it is hoping love wins over fear—for him, for others, and for me. Love is walking away from that experience *feeling*. Feeling impacted, changed, and vulnerable. That's love.

In the process of learning how to be a counselor, we all hear the phrase "unconditional positive regard" over and over again. It's a beautiful phrase, and it's a phrase rooted in love. The very nature of showing unconditional positive regard is love. And as therapists, we search and search for words to make love clinical. We search for clinical words to make it less like love, to make it less what it is. Why must we mask it and make it complicated, coded, and hidden? We do that as counselors because love is intimate and deep and vulnerable. And complicated. Love is ever so complicated for some of us and for many of our clients. And the ingredients of the deep work in counseling often require us to push ourselves, check ourselves, and be open to feedback, learning, and growth. It requires us to be honest, self-aware, and reflective of our own needs, desires, longings, triggers, and fears. It requires that we examine the role of love in our own relationships, past and present.

This Is Too Complex For My Brain Today

A part of me feels disappointed and frustrated that I also have to say love is not countertransference in regard to this tearful man in my office. Love is not needing love or appreciation from him. Love is not depending on our clients to meet our emotional needs. Love is not unhealthy, unsafe, or unfiltered.

As you read in chapter two, we all have ghosts that haunt us, and the good work of a counselor requires us to begin addressing those ghosts. Especially, since that is often the work of a counselor, unpacking and unraveling ways in which love has helped, healed, or hurt us. For us and for our clients, love can be a complicated topic.

With long histories of trauma and abuse paired with a world that rarely talks about mutuality and love, it comes as no surprise that the topic of love can be burdened with layers of confusion and difficulty. Unfortunately, love hasn't always meant safety and security for some of us and for some of our clients. Many of us, myself included, have ghosts from our past that confuse love with other things that are quite the opposite of love and create skewed perspectives of what it means to love and be loved by another. It might even feel "too complex for your brain" to think about how the two can come together. And reader, if that's you, it's okay. I see you. It's okay if you are uncomfortable talking about the concept of love with respect to the work of a counselor. It's okay if the thought of that scares you. It's okay if you have more alarm bells about it than you do warm, fuzzy feelings. You are not alone in wondering how on earth you might ever get to a point of even feeling like this is an important chapter in a book about the heart of counseling.

Let me tell you, readers, as much as I am advocating for love here, I struggled as I wrote this chapter. A lot. There were tears as I reached into my heart to find the words to write about love. I wrote the whole chapter and then realized it was all about "what not to do" rather than a message of "lean into love." Instead, I wrote about what to lean away from. The caution signs and disclaimers started to take over. And while they are important, they're only part of the story. I got scared, too. As much as I want to tell you to bring in love, it also scares me—sometimes a lot and sometimes just a little bit. I threw that version of the chapter away. One big highlight and delete.

It's scary to sink into what love looks like in the spaces where I invite it. It's vulnerable. It's honest. It's uncharted. We didn't learn this. There were no discussions about it in graduate school. I haven't read any articles about it. I'm paving this trail here through the forest, and I can't go over it, I can't go under it, I'm going through it. And it requires me to look at myself, my choices, my life, and my mistakes and realize that I, too, have work to do here. And that feels very exposing. As much as I want to have arrived here in this chapter for you and lead you to the "other side," I'm inviting you to link arms with me as we traverse this bridge together. As we explore together what it *could* look like and *might* feel like.

Love As Guide

Love drives a lot of our therapeutic work, and it's incredibly crucial that it does. Just today, I was meeting with a supervision group of amazing women who are moments away from licensure. Collectively, they are spending countless (actually, quite meticulously counted) hours with clients in the throes of trauma and grief. They tend to the hearts of those with eating disorders, marital infidelity, job loss, infertility, the loss of a young child, and with debilitating anxiety and overwhelming depression. Every day. Every week. Every month. All year.

Today, the group showed up to supervision with a blanket of exhaustion over their bodies. This work of a counselor is hard work. They felt confused, lost, overwhelmed, and spent. Many of them felt stuck in a place of frustration and lack of progress with their clients, and the burden on these counselors felt significant. The room felt dark and heavy. Collectively, we acknowledged this, normalized the heaviness of the work, and validated the burdens we carry. In the somber reflections, one of the women, with tears in her eyes, said quietly, almost as if to herself at first, "But I *love* this work." The emotion became more raw for her, and she said again, and you could hear the emotion catching in her throat, "I *love* this work. I really do." She paused,

"I *love* this even when it's hard. I *love* my clients. I *love* what I do."
A collective nodding spread across the group, the dichotomy of
the burden and the intense love for the work, so prominent.

> I have seen people moved and changed by love. I
> have experienced people inspired by love in ways
> that truth, fear, or shame cannot inspire. Counseling,
> by its very nature, is really just loving well.

Many of us deeply love this work. We feel called to this
work. We feel motivated by this work. Even when it's exhausting and burdensome and dark and overwhelming, there's still a
love for the work, for tending to the hearts and souls of others.
It's this love that guides us as counselors. Henri Nouwen writes,
"Each step of love is like a candle burning in the night. It doesn't
take the darkness away, but it guides us through the darkness."[4]
There's a love for being with others in their darkness. There's
still the candle burning, shining love in the darkest of days. Honoring the sacredness of the conversation with the women, I whispered, "What is it you love?" With quiet reverence, they shared:

"I love watching people discover a new part of themselves."
"I love being with people as a source of comfort."
"I love experiencing change as a result of vulnerability."
"I love growing alongside them."
"I love helping people feel safe."
"I love my clients."
"I love holding the tenderness of tears and the sacredness
of love."

Yes, we can talk about love in counseling. Yes, we can love
what we do. Yes, we can love our clients (in a boundaried way).

Yes, we can love some clients and not every client. And when we honor how love is a part of the process, we can work to love ourselves and our own pain and healing needs in the process as well.

I have seen people moved and changed by love. I have experienced people inspired by love in ways that truth, fear, or shame cannot inspire. Counseling, by its very nature, is really just loving well. We counselors are in the profession of learning to love and walking with others as they do the same. Counseling is the practice of drawing close to people in a way that opens their hearts to us, to others, and to love. And this kind of love creates a tremendous influence. Love is like water, gentle and crushing in its ability to create movement. American philosopher Dallas Willard wrote, "The most important thing about the care of souls is that you must love them."[5] The movement of love is active—a noun and a verb all in one. Love is loving.

Love As An Inspiration

I remember being changed and inspired by love fairly recently in my work as a counselor. I had been providing counseling to a married couple for over a year, and they had grown considerably. One particular week, we spent a session reflecting on our work together, things they had learned, and areas of growth in their connection and the expression of feeling connected. It was one of those warm, fuzzy sessions where we all felt affirmed about our work together. At the closing of the session, the wife, who is especially expressive of her feelings and thanksgiving, turned to me and shared, "Love you, friend." My brain immediately lit up with alarm bells, flashing lights, and neon blinking lights yelling, "Caution!" I was flooded with, "Oh no, what I have done wrong to make you misunderstand that not only am I not your *friend*, but *love* is not a part of what we're doing here. Sure, love between the two of you, but not me!" Readers, I've been doing this work for a long time, and I still started instantly sweating, wanting to run, and feeling like I had massively screwed up and miscommunicated what our relationship was about. I panicked.

Like a bolt of lightning, I saw myself losing my license, the licensing board driving over, putting handcuffs on me, and dragging me to counselor jail. But here's the reality: she expressed genuine love, care, compassion, and thanksgiving for me and for our work. She recognized my gifts and wanted to make sure I felt how much she appreciated me. Maybe even loved me. She wasn't weird about it. She didn't reach out for a huge embrace while we confessed our love for each other. She saw me and I saw her, human to human, heart to heart, and expressed love. And, friends, it was beautiful (after I got over my panic and shoved her out my door and fell on the couch to process my feelings). The sentiment, the expression, the love, is beautiful. I left that day feeling like maybe my client taught *me* something about love. Maybe my client was saying to me what I had been saying to that boy friend many years ago...that maybe it's okay to separate "I love you as a beautiful human" from "I love you, client, and I want to share my life stories with you and make you depend on me for all the things."

Maybe as we learn to navigate love in life, in relationships, and in the counseling space, we can learn to love others and ourselves well through loving clients. I think we don't really *teach* love as much as we *do* it. Model it. Learn from our clients about love. And maybe it's not from a blurring of boundaries. Perhaps it's actually easier to love the worst parts of ourselves by loving those same parts in our clients. Our work with others heals parts of us that need healing, too. And that's okay. And that's love: unconditional positive regard for ourselves through others.

> Love abounds in the counseling space whether we realize it or not, and part of our movement from being burdened to becoming is living loved and helping our clients to do the same. Love is the bridge from being burdened to ultimate belonging.

There is a gut-level tenderness to myself, an unconditional loving that translates into speaking kindly and compassionately, tuning my ear to the hurting parts inside me, that lets me do the same for my clients. Love to me, love to them. And I am inspired to love myself more so I can love them. Perhaps love is unconditionally seeking the best interest of another no matter what they do to you. The client who triangulated me. The client who was, honestly, beyond what I could offer. The client who scared me. The client who frustrated me. The client who withdrew from me. As I love them, I love those parts of me and practice loving myself well. Then I heal, too. That's magical and artful. Literal creation and the undoing of chaos.

Perhaps love is letting *myself* be unconditionally loved by another. Letting myself be the recipient of someone else's undoing of chaos. As a therapist, I don't think I can love unloved. I think loving comes from a place of being loved. Reader, counselor, friend, love is both strong and calm like water, scary and sacred, hurtful and healing, lonely and shared. Love abounds in the counseling space whether we realize it or not, and part of our movement from being burdened to becoming is living loved and helping our clients do the same. Love is the bridge from being burdened to ultimate belonging.

As I was concluding the writing process of this chapter on love, on leaning into love, I took my daughter and a few of her friends to a local pizzeria. As we were leaving, just outside the front door on the busy sidewalk was a leaf in the perfect shape of a heart. I picked it up and giggled at the perfect timing of ending my chapter on love and the Earth blessing me with the reminder for you and me, reader, to look for love. Amid the busyness and hustle of our world, be on the lookout. On the streets and in the coffee shop and in the counseling room. Look for love in our clients, in the counseling space, in our work, in the hard dark days of counseling, and in the days that feel peaceful and life-giving. Look for love in ourselves and in the hearts of others. Where do you see love? Where would you like to see love that you don't quite yet? Where do you see love in counseling? What might you call it other than love, and at what cost?

Find the signs of hearts in *your* path, dear counselor. Look for love, and when you find it, lean in.

CHAPTER FIVE

Created for Connection

I stood on the side of the road, wearing my Girls on the Run[1] coach t-shirt, waiting for the hot and sweaty preteen girls with determination on their faces to round the corner. Over 500 girls were running, each with a running buddy in tow, and I was geared up to shout, cheer, and scream for them along the way in hopes it would provide a much-needed source of inspiration, connection, and determination. I was there, along with many other spectators, to fight for them to cross that finish line. To fight for them to believe they could finish. To fight for them to see their value, their worth, and their accomplishment when they believe in themselves.

There I was, screaming, ringing my cowbell, and offering high fives to the runners that passed by. As I offered high fives, these preteen girls moved from the opposite side of the road to seek one out. And so did their adult running buddies. Adults crossed the road for high fives as much as kids did. All of them with a smile on their face and energy radiating from their desire for this connection point. Human-to-human magical energy through the form of touch. Sit in that for a moment. Picture these humans, ages ranging from eight to sixty years old, faces lighting up, smiles growing, with sounds of encouragement, crossing a road to get a high five from a stranger. Think about how often we need high fives from people standing on the sidelines of life, or the encouragement we need from others as we navigate the twists and turns on the route we run every single day. Consider what it would feel like at the end of a busy day, headed to the grocery store for dinner ingredients, passing by signs that read, "You've got this!" or "I'm proud of you," or "You're doing amazing." I might be a little lighter and a little more encouraged during the routine task.

We need people. We need others to ring cowbells, to offer high fives, to hold up signs of encouragement written with glitter markers. We, you and me, need others to share in our triumphs and in our hard spaces and to read the signs of encouragement. I want this for you, dear reader. I am here along your journey, cheering for you and holding up glittery signs in the form of chapters.

> Think about how often we need high fives from people standing on the sidelines of life, or the encouragement we need from others as we navigate the twists and turns on the route we run every single day.

I desperately want you to hear my screaming, feel my support, hear the cowbell ringing, and feel my high five as you pass by. I want to be this for you, reader. I want you to see me holding up a sign for *you*, reminding *you* of your worth, your value, your purpose. I want you to feel my hope for you and my belief in you. And as much as I want that for you, my words can only support you so much. Even though there is a heartbeat behind the words on these pages, belonging to a fellow counselor named Michelle, most of you don't know me. I am the unnamed coach on the side of the road cheering for you, helping you feel motivated for the duration of the current run.

And, dear sojourning friend, you need your people. It's as simple and complicated as that. You need your people. The ones who greet you at the finish line with hugs and congratulations and cheer you along your own races. While I'm happy to be your cheerleader along the way on these pages, you also need someone there for you when you finish this book and set it on your shelf or pass it along to someone else who needs a high five along their path. This chapter is your encouragement to find your finish line people.

Created To Seek

We are all created for connection. We are hard-wired to need others,[2] to depend on others, and to be in relationship with others, ideally with healthy people in satisfying relationships. As therapists, we know this, and it is the foundation of our work. I saw this in the 5K. People need people. We need others so deeply to cheer for us, to shout for us, and to be there for us when we feel like we can't go any further. Clients come to us—they go to *you*, another human being—to seek healing, perspective, togetherness, compassion, and guidance. It's one thing when we offer a high five to passersby, but it's a whole other thing to actively seek them out. And clients seek us out as counselors. When we are young children, we need people. When we are adults, we need people. You need people. I need people.

Scientists, researchers, and counselors have been working to prove this fact in various ways for over a hundred years. A well-known psychological research project[3] in the 1950s conducted by Harry Harlow demonstrated this with primates. In one part of the study, Harlow took infant monkeys from their biological mothers and gave them two surrogate mothers: one a construction of wire and wood, and the second a fake monkey mother covered in foam rubber and soft terry cloth. He wanted to know if the baby monkeys would prefer one over the other, one cold and wiry and one warmer and soft. Spoiler alert: they picked the terry cloth mother. Even when presented with a new and scary situation, the monkeys would literally run to the terry cloth "mother" for comfort.

Let's slow down here a bit. When faced with fear, a monkey will seek comfort from something. *And*, it will seek out wire covered in soft terry cloth over something more innate. A primate's instinct, their wiring, our wiring, *your wiring*, is to seek "another" in a scary situation. Our basic primate instincts are to need others and to *seek* others. Our core need is to seek connection. Our core desire is to seek connection. To cross the road for a high five. To light up when we are encouraged. To find connection when we feel alone. And yes, I know, many of our ghosts have taught us along the way that this isn't true, that people aren't safe, and that we are safer on our own. Attachment theory supports that these deep-wired longings teach us to form safe, caring bonds with other beings in order to have healthy nervous systems. Secure attachment creates neural pathways that are imperative for the healthy functioning of our brains. Our biology is literally intertwined with the natural yearnings of our hearts. We are born with an innate desire to connect. We are literally created to be relational beings who need others to function well. You, too, counselor. You too.

Connection For Counselors

As therapists, we generally know this to be true for our clients, but it may be less obvious or seem less important for ourselves. I think we counselors are much better at seeing and nurturing this need with our clients than we are at following it ourselves. "Do as I say, not as I do." We know that the power of the relationship in therapy is an integral piece of the healing and change process. But we can translate that outside of the therapy room, too. In a basic sense, we need others. An extension of the last chapter, leaning into love, means building relationships and connection with others. When we have a job like ours, we need to lean into love with others. We all need someone to walk with us as we walk with others. We need this when we don't understand an assignment in graduate school. You need this when graduate school or counseling feels too hard, too scary, too lonely, or requires too much internal stretching.

> Our basic human instincts are to need others and to seek others. Our core need is to seek connection. Our core desire is to seek connection.

We need this when we feel confused about how to show up as a therapist in a role-play. We need this when we feel scared about seeing our first client. We need to lean into love when our first (or one-hundredth) client feels like too much. And we need this when we're out in the field doing the work, day after day, and feel joy and confidence and want to share that with someone who understands that the good days are *really* good. Like that time when I so desperately longed for someone to celebrate with when my client said, with tears in her eyes, "Your compassion has changed my life." Or when another client said,

"My wife must not care about our marriage if she chose you as our counselor," and I wanted to run out of the room and cry in the bathroom. We need others when the bad days are *really* discouraging. We need people who know better when we tell them we're "fine" and give us a hug, bring us a coffee, or text us later with a "Hey, I'm thinking about you; how are you really doing?" Or the special few who really know who we can call up, share our tears with, and they gently hold our tears, our words, and our longings. And they see us. Deeply. And they tell us, "I got you. You didn't mess up. You can do this. Let me tell you what I know to be true about you."

Therapy can be an isolating experience. We sit all day with others who are with us for a short time and then leave our space. Counseling is not intended to be an equal two-way connection where they care for us as much as we care for them. Therapists tolerate isolation, anxiety, depression, loss, grief, and frustration. We spend all day in intimacy with others, but in ways that are not intended to meet our own needs for intimacy. Dear counselor, counseling is not meant to be practiced alone. We are not intended to walk this journey of counseling alone and isolated from others. Although I'm sure isolation is what our ghosts would prefer.

Connecting With Angels

Sometimes, based on our past experiences and the ghosts that linger around us, it's scary to lean into love and build relationships of trust. Meet Jessica. Jessica has ghosts. Like many of us, Jessica's ghosts linger. Some shout, and some dance around and tell her lies about herself, her worth, and her skills as a counselor. Jessica was a graduate student looking for an internship, weighing the pros and cons of various internship experiences, client populations, and client hour availability. I interviewed Jessica for an internship at the clinic where I served as the Clinical Director. We quickly developed rapport, we connected, we laughed, and we shared similar goals about counseling and the supervisory relationship. She was a great fit for our clients, for supervision with me, and for learning.

But, like some of you, Jessica was scared. She could see me and knew that I could see her: her growth edges, her needs, her soft spots, and her heart for the work. And Jessica got too scared and turned down the internship. And you know what I did (which I had never done before and may never do again)? I told her I thought maybe she was wrong. I pursued her. I told her what I saw in her. I told her I chose her. And you know what she did? *She changed her mind.*

Relationships and connections matter. And, as you might predict, sometimes she still wants to run away. Her ghosts tell her to run from scary and new things. And I keep grabbing her hand and telling her to try. I stand, armored alongside her, and fight her ghosts with her, reminding her that she is enough, she is equipped, and she is more ready than her ghosts tell her she is. I remind her that she is brave, and over time, she believes this more and more. Soon, she begins to explore, adventure, and bring her authentic self to her work. She tames some of those ghosts, and she learns to go "through it" rather than over, under, or around her fears. She faces the ghosts, but she doesn't do it alone—not at first. She battles those ghosts in relationship with another human being. She faces her fears, one at a time, with a safe person by her side. We all need someone to stand beside us, armored against our ghosts, and face our fears, doubts, and insecurities alongside us. We all need someone in our lives to scream their lungs out for us when we round the corner on our run through life to hold up that glittery sign that says, "You can do this!" You deserve this.

> Hey, I see you. Please stop running. There's healing for you here.

And while I am wired for connection just like each of you, my own ghosts have told me to run, too. Or told me to seek connection from a place of codependency. And I have. I've dodged and ducked from points of connection, and I still do. But I've done some work here. While I'm not finished with that work, I was able to see Jessica and see her running away and say, "Hey, I see you. Please stop running. There's healing for you here." And I was able to do that because of *angels*. Similar to the ghosts that haunt us, we have angels as well. Rather than haunt us, these angels protect, guard, and encourage us. They hold our figurative hand, like I did with Jessica and like others have done with me, and say *stay*. Be here.

Thirty years after Fraiberg introduced the idea of ghosts in the nursery, another brilliant soul, Alicia Liberman, wrote about these angels, suggesting that in addition to the ghosts, we have angels in the nursery.[4] Wait. Let's take that in right here. Those ghost stories are pretty haunting. "Now you're telling me there are angels, too?" Yes, reader, I am. You have angels from the nursery, too. Thank goodness. As you might imagine, the idea is that when we are infants, if we are surrounded by sources of love and care, we build inner resources of love, safety, and belonging. These become angels that carry us through difficult times, give us strength when we are weak, and guide us through storms.

Just like the ghosts that can be formed from infancy into adulthood, angels are the same. They dance and float around us, protecting us from negativity, imposter syndrome, and insecurities. These angels are our protectors. They are our guides and encouragers. They show up when we feel overwhelmed or stuck or scared. If we did not have these during childhood, secure attachment research tells us we can find these later in life and cultivate an inner experience of love and belonging through these angels. Jessica can tell you that, too. These angels can stand beside us and fight against the impact of our ghosts. Remind us of our worth. Draw us to connect with healthy others. The angels remind us that healed people heal others. They show us that we can do hard things, even when it's scary.

These angels come in all forms: a teacher, a counselor, a coach, a friend, or a significant other. While we don't all experience angels from the nursery or our childhood home, often, these angels show up in the presence of another around us throughout our lives. We need these angels. If we do not have them, this becomes a crucial aspect of surviving and thriving in the field of counseling.

Just like in the previous section about ghosts, I had a graduate student who would have disagreed if I had said to him, "We all have angels." He would share that while he believes *others* have angels in the nursery, his life up until this point has been pretty horrific, especially his infancy and childhood. He would share that he never really had a home or a nursery, never mind angels in those spaces. And the ghosts have followed him ever since and chased away any angels that may have attempted to get close. And maybe you feel similar. Maybe you don't feel like you've ever had angels that protect your heart or a group of people around you reflecting back your worth and value. If this is you, sweet human, I believe you. I see you. I know this space feels lonely. I know everything feels different for you, and that isolates you even further. I know you've never really felt chosen. I know you've never experienced someone at that finish line waiting for you or even that stranger along the side of the road with a glittery sign. I want you to know there's still time. You haven't missed your chance. Just like you need people, people need *you*.

> These angels can stand beside us and fight against the impact of our ghosts. Remind us of our worth. Draw us to connect with healthy others. The angels remind us that healed people heal others. They show us that we can do hard things, even when it's scary.

Maybe any angels around you right now seem really insignificant. Maybe it's just Sam from Trader Joe's who asks how your dog is by name every time you see him. Maybe right now, it's the woman who sits next to you in class and always brings an extra granola bar and offers it to you. Or maybe it's Jeff, the mailman who asks how your day is going and really seems to mean it when he asks. Maybe one of your angels was the German teacher when you were in high school who let you hang out in her classroom during lunch so you wouldn't eat alone. Maybe one of your angels was the track coach who happily sat on the bleachers with you after practice when your parents forgot to pick you up. Again. Maybe it was the kindergarten teacher who snuck you a box of crayons when they saw you didn't bring any school supplies like the rest of the kids.

Some angels are in our physical lives for a short time or in a small, seemingly insignificant way, but their imprints can stay with us for years or even decades, battling our ghosts. Sometimes they don't even have names, or have names we have long forgotten. Angels have shown up this way for you, and you've done this for others, too. There are interactions you've had with others that have impacted them. You have become other people's angel without even knowing it and left a permanent tattoo on them, potentially forever. Simply by showing up for them at that time and in that way, touching their heart permanently.

You see, these relationships are crucial to who we become. Angels remind us that connection is part of our healing, health, and ability to reach for others who are hurting. Angels show us that counseling matters and it changes people—it changes us. Angels in our lives show us that connection matters. Connection is the very *heart of counseling*. This is what it is all about. Connection. Without the content of this chapter, we don't have counseling, we don't have ghosts, we don't have angels, and we don't have love to lean into. The heartbeat of our work as counselors is all about connection. We are literally wired to be in relationship with others. And because of these ghosts and the harm they've caused, sometimes we have to fight pretty hard to create, become, and model healthy connections. And reader, you are so deeply worth that fight.

The angels that enter our lives or that we intentionally invite into our lives create corrective emotional experiences. I think of these corrective experiences as creating deer trails out in a field. Our negative experiences become so ingrained in us that a clear and well-worn pathway develops. We can easily find it, hop on it, put our heads down, and travel that pathway. When we reach for someone for safety, protection, or encouragement, our negative game-trail brain pathway tells us "danger," "not safe." But these angels take our hand, and rather than taking the road most traveled, they start a new pathway, a less traveled path through the field.

And when we get to that same crossroad the next time, our angels take our hand, providing a corrective emotional and safe experience that allows us to trust a little bit more that this new pathway leads to something different, something better. These angels literally become our guides to connection, trust, and safety. One step at a time through the dark and new pathway. Hand in hand. Heart to heart. In it together.

When we develop healthy relationships with healthy (or mostly healthy) people, we begin to experience a safe haven, a place to turn when we experience distress. The road to this safe haven develops over time, and only after enough reaffirming, encouraging experiences have occurred for us to start believing they're true. When we have a secure base with these angels in our lives, we also begin to feel safe, assured, and curious to explore the world. And as we get more confident in this relationship, it helps us to do this with genuine authenticity and curiosity.

Core Heart People

These safe haven angels are a precious few. They are the ones we trust with our insecurities, our doubts, our growth edges, our dreams, and our nightmares. Maybe this is one person for you, or maybe it's five people. These are your core heart people. As much as I would love to be a heart person for everyone, I can't do that. But I so deeply want this for you, reader. I want you to have safe haven angels. So, I'm going to beg, boss, and plead with you to show up for yourself in three important ways in this chapter.

The first is to take a moment right now and cut out a little heart. Grab a piece of paper near you—or, heck, cut out a little corner of the book page right here—and cut out a one-inch heart. The size matters because this isn't for all your next-level heart people; this is the main, real-deal, safe haven heart people. Go slow here; be thoughtful. Sink into your needs, your safety, your heart, your connection. Who is that safe haven for you? Write their name(s) on this little core heart. There was a time in my life when my heart had one person on it. There are times in my life when my heart has four names on it. And that's okay. This heart doesn't have to be the one heart forever; it can shift and change over time.

Some of you might be thinking, "But I don't have *anyone*. I don't have any name I can write on that little heart." And for you, this exercise makes you feel even more alone than before. For you, let me wonder with you: is there really nobody, or have your ghosts just told you that for so long that you believe them? Maybe. But maybe not. Maybe you do have someone who can be that person. Write their name down. Identify that relationship. Fight against those ghosts right here and right now. For others of you, maybe it's true that you really don't have any-one right now. I see you and I believe you, and your loneliness matters. This is part of your work, right here. This is important work. You need to fight against those ghosts and get someone on that list. Maybe not today, but work to add a name to that heart. Maybe it's your therapist for now. But invite those angels in to help you see your value in being in relationship with others.

Now, take that heart and tuck it away in a book, a wallet, or a drawer. Keep it. Know it. Feel these people in your heart. These people on this heart are your people who reflect truth to you, who know your heart and intentions, hope for the best for you, and love you fiercely.

These core heart people can be an important part of protecting us as well. A few years ago, I was supervising a counselor working towards licensure. She had a particularly rough session where the client shared some really critical, uninvited feedback. Not just the "growth opportunity" type of feedback but the soul-crushing, gut-wrenching, downright *mean* feedback. She was crushed, ready to quit being a counselor altogether. Have you ever felt that way? If not, you will. I share that not to scare you but to normalize it for you. And to get you ready, armed with angels at the ready, listed right there on that heart you just made (or intend to make). I asked this counselor if this client's name was written on her little heart. Of course not! The people on this heart are your truth-tellers. These are the people whose opinion really matters, and when you don't measure up, don't get the A, get fired by a client, or get fired from a job, they are the safe haven people who love you no matter what. When you feel lies or ghosts creeping in, ask them to speak truth to you. When a client shares with you what a horrible person and counselor you are, ask your safe haven people to speak truth to you, about you. And, please, love your core heart person well.

Reach For Connection

We all have layers of relationships with people in our lives. We have layers of people in relationship with us, and, like a stone dropping in a pond, the further out the ripple goes, the less connected they are with the core of who we are. These core heart people are in the center; they are the person or people who matter the very most to you. The next ripples, as they move away from your core heart people, are people who are close to you, then less close, all the way out to those you associate with but are not close to your heart. But the people in the first ripple are important, too. They aren't quite your core person, but they are people who matter significantly to you. They are people in our lives who support, encourage, trust, and love us. These are people who know you and your heart well; they genuinely care about you and are invested in you. They don't have to know counselor-you or counseling, but they know your angels (and many of them are your angels), and they know something about your ghosts, too.

Here's my second bossy/pleading invitation for you to show up for yourself: identify this next layer of people. Make a mental list of at least three. Maybe these are classmates, colleagues, professors, or friends. Look at your texts on your phone right now. Who do you text the most? Text them right now and say:

"Will you do me a favor? Will you describe me in 3-5 words?"

Don't think about it too much; just do it. Copy, paste, send. Show up for yourself today. Because I don't want to ask you to do anything I am not also willing to do, I reached out to eight of my people and asked them to describe me in 3-5 words. And you know what? They showed up for me. They reflected my tenderness, my dedication, my authenticity, and my fierce love for others. And as much as I felt like I knew those things about myself, I cried. Hearing those words from my heart people made me feel so seen. I (once again) realized I need to hear these affirmations more than I think I do. Their carefully chosen words reminded me of many of my *whys*, my value, my strengths, my purpose. Each highlighting slightly different perspectives.

Our heart people are incredibly important and, in some ways, are just waiting for the opportunity to reflect back to us what they see. Part B of this ask is to write these words down. Hang them on the fridge, behind your computer at work, or tuck them somewhere private and secure. But write them down. Reference them. Look at them. Take them in.

I once worked with a client who struggled to see her value and her strengths during a difficult divorce. While I had been reminding her how strong she was and had used a lot of adjectives to describe how I could see this strength show up in her daily life, I was only one heart person. I invited her to reach out to her people and ask them to describe her in 3-5 words. This beautiful human walked through the door at her next counseling appointment, crying before she even sat down.

She gently tossed a handful of papers beside me and sat in silence, crying yet communicating so much. Her people showed up for her. They showed up for her in beautiful and affirming ways. They saw her: her heart, her hurt, her resilience, her tenderness, her compassion, her pain. They saw it all. Suddenly, she went from feeling so alone to feeling so seen. As we pored over the words, I asked her to reflect on themes that she felt in these reflections. She saw strength, perseverance, and fierceness. One friend described this as her "Lioness," and the client beamed with pride. She shared how she felt like this was deep inside her, hidden away from herself and from everyone else, covered by fears, doubts, and insecurities. When others reflected this back to her, she began to feel it. To own it. She went out and bought a lioness mug and earrings. She started taking up space in her life like a lioness. When people who knew her in several different contexts reflected the same thing back, she let it settle into places in her heart where she didn't let it before. It gave her the confidence to believe the words. It helped her see herself again.

Pursuing Connection

These words are an important part of connection. Connection is built; it doesn't just magically happen. It takes work, intentionality, and persistence. My third invitation is for you to create *connection*. This is a big one. This invitation comes from a place of knowing. I know what it feels like to feel lonely. I'm familiar with what it feels like to be a fierce introvert yet also have a deep desire to feel known and seen. And for us counselors, I know what it feels like to be the giver and rarely the receiver. This is a big ask, friend. It can be scary to reach for others, fearful that they won't reach back.

If you are a student, I encourage you to reach for others. Meet people. Develop a network. Exchange phone numbers. Bring an extra granola bar or banana to share with your neighbor in class. Learn their name. Learn their kids or dogs' names. Reach out for help on an assignment. Ask them about APA. Lovingly complain about the professor's long syllabus. Start somewhere.

And then share about how stuck you feel. And then about how imposter syndrome is becoming overpowering. Ask to meet for coffee. Plan a study date. The people you surround yourself with in these first few years of this career *matter*. They need you as much as you need them. I promise. Help create group supervision as a place of safety and trust. Seek it and co-create it, whether in the classroom itself or outside of it.

Create a community of heart people, of angels, who help you feel like you belong, who care for you as a person behind the counselor chair. Dear student, as a professor, I've seen literally hundreds of long-term safe havens built in grad school. Some call it trauma-bonding. Call it whatever you want to call it. Find your heart people. They're already there, waiting to be found.

> Create a community of heart people, of angels, who help you feel like you belong, who care for you as a person behind the counselor chair.

If you are a counselor, I encourage you to reach for others. Being a counselor can be so lonely. For everyone. But as counselors, we feel lonely in our own little corner of the world, hoping to connect with other people who are lonely in their own little corner of the world. We are people who need people, assuming that others don't need us as much as we need them. But they do. You do. I do. Connection requires work. You know those people you connected with in grad school, and then you went your separate ways? Text them! Those colleagues you met at the conference and kind of connected with? Meet them for coffee! Stop waiting for "someday we'll do that" and do it *today*. Create a monthly meet-up for counselors. Coffee corner, book club, "wine down" time, happy hour. I don't care what you call it; just get together. During the pandemic, I created a monthly Zoom meet-up, called it "counselor connection," and had *so many* people show up, just longing to stay connected with others, because I longed to stay connected with others. Turn those longings and needs for connection into actual connection. Keep your heart people. Keep them!

If you are a supervisor or a professor, I encourage you to reach for others. Thank you for picking up this book and reading it, taking in reminders of what it was like to be a beginner. Model for your students, interns, and supervisees how much we need others. Develop a connection with them. See them and let them see you. Be a human with them. Let your students and interns know you care for them and that they teach you and help you continue to grow. Help them to find and keep their own heart people. Build them. Create them. Empower them. Surround yourself with colleagues you respect and admire to help improve your own work and leadership. I affirm the work you do every day. Love your heart people who helped get you here.

We all need others. We need the heart people and the more special few who are your core heart people. We need these finish line people. When we experience genuine connection, when we are in a safe and secure relationship with people we trust, we are more willing and safe to risk being vulnerable and authentic. Our process of "becoming" feels less scary and lonely. Developing this community is courageous and brave, and I affirm you for stepping into this process of connection.

At any point in your story, you can develop angels. At any point in your story, you can create heart people. You need community. You need to gather people who will tell you that the things you are doing matter. That you matter, that your work matters. That your words matter and that the world needs *you*, not some version of you, *just you*.

In real-time here, as I was finishing this chapter, I texted one of my heart people to share the struggle of writing a chapter that felt so seminal to the heart of the book, and hoping so deeply that it resonates with you, reader, in the ways I long for it to. And she shared with me these very words:

"I'm so, so proud of you for showing up today. You showed up authentically, tears and all. You are creating a gift, no, *birthing* a gift that's already inside you, and you are showing up *willing to go through labor pains to get there*. You are so courageous."

Reader, this is the kind of community I want for you. One that shows up in these heart spaces and reflects back to you, "I'm so proud of you" and "You are so courageous." That lifts you up when you're filled with doubts or insecurities or when you just need loving words of encouragement. When I open myself to vulnerability, a beautiful community fills in the gaps of doubt with love and connection. Yours will, too, when you invite them in.

CHAPTER SIX

Stop Pretending to be a Therapist

"It takes courage to grow up and become who you really are."
~E.E. Cummings[1]

There's an aged man standing in the middle of the jungle, dressed in a business suit, surrounded by children wearing dirt-stained, play-ridden clothing, with jungle swings, tree houses, and creations all around. This man, Peter Banning, is not familiar with these surroundings. He's lost, confused, and clearly not made for this nonsense. He's just been taken from his business world, where he is an unimaginative, workaholic lawyer and a dad of two young children. His archenemy, Captain Hook, has kidnapped his children, and Tinkerbell has brought Peter Banning here to Neverland to fight to get his children back.

However, Peter Banning doesn't believe he used to be Peter Pan. He doesn't believe he used to be silly or have food fights with make-believe magical food. He doesn't believe he used to fly. And neither do the kids who never grew up in the magical Neverland.

So there he stands, in his suit and tie, so far from who he was when he was last there. The person who took his place when he left, Rufio, definitely doesn't believe this is the same person who was full of life, playfulness, and love; he has grown up and become unrecognizable. So, he draws a literal line in the sand and says, "If any of you said this here scug ain't Peter Pan, cross the line." All of the children cross the line, stating their disbelief that Peter Pan still lives in the body of professional, adult Peter Banning. Peter himself crosses the line; he, too, doesn't believe it. He doesn't remember the parts of himself that giggled and played and created.

Everyone crosses except for one young boy. This sweet little child tenderly walks around Peter, touching Peter's knees as he circles him, gazing at him with great curiosity and wonder. He pulls Peter down to his knees so they are eye to eye. He takes off his glasses and places his two small hands on either side of Peter's face. With small, youthful hands tenderly cupping Peter's worn and tired face, the child gently pushes and pulls at his cheeks and forehead, looking for signs that the Peter he knows is still in there.

Then, all at once, his eyes light up, and a smile of fondness and recognition stretches across his face. "Oh, there you are, Peter!" he shares. The rest of the children run over, smiles of recognition spread across the group of children as they run their fingers through his curly hair and tug on his wrinkled skin to find the magical Peter Pan underneath the years of "growing up."

This touching scene from the movie *Hook*[2] reminds me a lot of you and me, reader. We grow up, we learn, we go to school, and then more school, and then more school, and we change and get impacted by what we learn. Sometimes, the person we become begins to be unrecognizable from the person we are inside. We work, we wear professional clothing, we learn, we run errands, and we complete tasks. We save money to buy bigger things and spend money on broken things. At some point, you or someone else draws a line in the sand. One side is your professional, responsible, parent, grown-up self or the professional life you *should* have, and on the other side of the line is your playful, flying, fighting, crowing self. We all need to find our way back to that person, or to integrate the two together, to remember who we are and the magic we possess. This chapter is one gigantic permission slip to discover, rediscover, find, and uncover the Peter Pan in you.

Where Did You Go?

I feel like part of my job as a professor is to find that Peter Pan in you. As a professor, I get to know students in a variety of contexts. I experience them in the classroom, I bump into them in the hallways and library, I watch them interact with fellow classmates, and I see them laughing at the coffee shop near campus with open books and full tummies. They bring snacks to class and share; they knit during lecture time, and make kids' birthday party invitations during break time. They use hushed voices in the back of the classroom, connecting over personal struggles. They are hard to herd back into the classroom after a break because they're laughing or crying and carrying on in the hallways. They're funny, loud, sarcastic, full of life, engaging, intentional, humble, brilliantly introverted, empathic, and deep. They're living their lives as Peter Pan.

Then, as beginners and learners, when asked to be a counselor, either in a role-play or in the practicum and internship experience, I watch you change. I watch you transform from Peter Pan, full of life and color and personality, to Peter Banning: professional, dutied, and responsible. It's like someone shut off the lights, or the room went from color to black and white. I watch the light drain from your face and the space. I feel deep sadness as I watch it happen. I want to grab your hand and keep you in Neverland. I want you to remember the ways you can fly and create and laugh, but the shadows come.

> You stop living in your humor
> You become serious
> There are no jokes
> Even the smiles change if that's possible
> The smiles become rare or forced
> A warm smile to a rehearsed smile
> You use words you don't usually use
> And you say them differently, too
> Calculated
> You sit differently, stiff and stoic
> The room feels heavy
> Clinical
> And filled with expectations
> And you leave
> I see it in your body
> I see it in your face
> I hear it in your words
> I hear it in your voice
> Your heart shifts, and
> You leave

The brilliant, introverted or extroverted, engaged, playful, funny, empathic, joyful, relaxed human that I have come to be quite fond of is gone. In a matter of seconds, the magic of Peter Pan in you disappears.

If I have the pleasure of being with you in this space, you know I stop you, mid role-play or video, and ask you:

Where did you go?
Why is your body like that?
Are you comfortable?
Why are you talking like that?
Where did YOU go?

And many of you look at me completely confused. Or sad. You don't even know your life left the space. You don't know you've become Peter Banning. You don't know your world changed from color to black and white.

"Where did you go?"

"I don't know."

I don't know, you say. And it's true. I believe you. When you are in new spaces, when your imposter syndrome kicks into high gear, and when your ghosts are hovering so close, you don't know where your authentic self goes. But it does. And you become unrecognizable, just like Peter Pan to those children. The gifts that drove you to this field, the ways you naturally connect with others, the truest parts of you that your angels work so desperately to remind you of are gone. We might know who we are outside of the counseling room, but we don't know who our authentic self is as a *counselor*.

Bringing our authentic selves into the therapy room is scary. We get nervous. We become afraid that those most authentic parts of us won't be welcomed. Or aren't professional. We are scared that our most authentic parts are maybe too much, or not enough, or maybe too reserved, or too bold, too sensitive, too different from what a therapist is, too something and too everything. So you put on layers of other people, of other theorists, of classmates and colleagues and professors and supervisors. We suit up like Peter Banning, hoping that professional layer will be enough. What remains is just a skeleton of the person that once was, a shadow of the life-filled Peter Pan.

And the saddest part of all is that those are the parts that your clients need the most. Those authentic pieces are the parts that clients connect deeply to. It's these parts of you that allow them to feel seen. The parts of you that clients feel, that develop safety and trust. Those are the parts that draw people in. These beautiful, authentic parts that those around you value and admire about you. About *you*, dear reader. Yes, *you*. The authentic self outside the counseling room is the same authentic self as a counselor. Is that easy to do? Nope. Is that something that comes naturally? Nope. And that's why I'm gifting you with one gigantic permission slip to bring your authentic self into the counseling room.

Put Down Your Notecards

A few years ago, I was preparing to speak at a conference about raising daughters. I was one of three speakers invited to speak at this event and share experiences, professionally and personally, that would teach and engage the audience. When the speakers met to prepare, the other amazing women could rattle off their main points, sub points, and sub-sub points of their speeches.

They could, off the top of their heads, share data and references to support these talking points.

I, on the other hand, had been practicing and rehearsing my talking points in the weeks leading up to this event and had a really hard time connecting the material with the outline. My imposter syndrome kicked into high gear. I'm not the rattle-off-research-and-authors-and-dates type. But they were, so I thought I probably should be, too. I was stuck in my head, thinking about the material but never really sinking into the heart space and *feeling* the message. It felt so rehearsed (because it was!), and as the day got closer, it felt like I was taking huge steps away from being my authentic and congruent self. I had become Peter Banning and had completely walked away from the creative Peter Pan in me.

> When we can bring our authentic selves to our stage, the counseling room, it encourages our clients to bring their authentic selves as well.

What I've learned about myself over the years is that I'm a more down-to-earth academic than one who recites dates and books and theories and theory origin stories (and people who can do that amaze and inspire me!). I'm much more confident as a speaker and supervisor when I'm my most authentic self, which actually feels both freeing and quite vulnerable. I am more my authentic self when I show up less prepared mentally but fully prepared in my heart.

In a lapse of judgment or frustration, I threw my notecards in the trash on top of the leftover spaghetti and slammed it shut. I moved away from expectations—mostly my own based on preconceived ideas of what I thought others expected of me. And I moved into a desire to show up in that space in all my glory: stumbling words, stories shared with emotion, and rambling thoughts. I cried. I searched. I begged. I wanted to quit. I wanted to tell them I wasn't able to make it. I was lost in a maze, trying to find my true self while surrounded by brilliant, intelligent, articulate women. I had no idea where my version of Peter Pan went or how to get back to that place. They didn't need me. What on earth could I even offer that they're not covering already with more poise and perfection than I could bring, even after countless attempts?

I ended up showing up to the speaking event feeling quite raw and unprepared, which was exactly what was needed to bring my most authentic self. I packed up an old suitcase with things from around my house and dropped it on stage, dumping out my "baggage," and spoke without a script, with true tears in my eyes about the baggage we bring into parenting. People connected with my heart, my tears, my creativity. They didn't know the notecards lingered in the trash at home; they didn't know the fear and anguish I felt in my preparation. They knew that I desperately wanted to connect with them, their hearts, their longings, and their deep desires to become a better parent for their young children.

When we can bring our authentic selves to our stage, the counseling room, it encourages our clients to bring their authentic selves as well. When we can put down the notecards, talking points, theory interventions, and brilliant next cued-up questions, we can attune to our own hearts and bring that into our spaces with others.

But Who Is My Authentic Self?

Sometimes, though, we don't have clarity about who our authentic self is. Sometimes, in our search to get back to our Peter Pan selves, we don't actually know how to get there or what it looks like when we've found our way back. I don't know about you, but I'm pretty good at being a chameleon, changing myself to fit my surroundings. So if someone were to ask me who my authentic self is, I might ask them in what context they're asking the question. You need a leader? Sign me up! You need me to go with the flow? I'm your gal. You need someone creative? You got it! You need a warm body and a wallflower? Here I am! I'm a professional chameleon—and I'm not particularly proud of it. Sometimes it's hard to know who we are at our core. And if we don't know who that is to begin with, it's hard to know how to bring that person to the counseling room. Many of us spend years trying to figure out who we are, especially who we are as a counselor. Sometimes we might not know, but others around us can help us figure it out. Guess what? That last chapter where I encouraged you to reach out to your heart people and write down the words they used to describe you? Those words matter here, too. Those are the words that help you find your way to your authentic self. Not because the value is in what others see in us but because they reflect back to us the things we show them. They are our reflections.

So, as you think about bringing your authentic self into the counseling room, when you think about sitting there, getting ready to be with people, think, "How would my closest friends describe me?" Sit with that question for a second. If they describe you as spunky, loving, and compassionate, are those parts of you in the counseling room? If they describe you as deep, nurturing, and adventurous, are those parts of you in the counseling room? Remember that being yourself (and your *self*) in that therapist chair is crucial, perhaps the most crucial part of how you show up with your clients. *You* are your greatest intervention. Who or how you show up in the room matters. Your authentic, silly, stumbling, easily confused, badass self.

A student recently shared these very words in a course reflection paper. She's learning that a counselor doesn't have to be a meek person who only ever listens and absorbs people's problems. She's learning that, professionally, she can be a "badass" as a therapist, which definitely fits with her most authentic self.

There are entire books and research about the self of the therapist, literal books about the therapist's self, about how important it is for the therapist to become part of the counseling process. For their personality, their hunches, their full self to be in the counseling room. We don't do therapy by inserting our hand into a black box, manipulating the clients, changing the dysfunctional patterns, and removing our hand from the change process happening in the box. We are *in* the box with them. All of us, whether we like it or not. Our selves being part of the counseling process is inevitable, crucial, and incredibly valuable. Your self—your true, authentic self—is a brilliant and necessary part of counseling.

> *You* are your greatest intervention.

Just a few weeks ago, I was talking with my Family Therapy class about their full selves being a part of the counseling process. A lively classroom discussion ensued about them being taught to sit stoically (with a silly acronym they've been taught), to remain emotionless, and to be sure to validate, reflect, and summarize. One of them shared that they were already tired of pretending to be Mr. Rogers[3] in all of their role-plays. Full stop. Hold the phone. What? I sat down on the table at the front of the room and asked them, "What parts of you do you shut off when you try to be Mr. Rogers? What crucial aspects of your beautiful selves are you scared to bring in?" And they shared:

> I've been wanting to get my nose pierced—can I do that as a therapist?
> Can I drink a glass of wine in a restaurant? What if a client sees me?
> I have ADHD, and I'm afraid they'll find out.
> Someone told me once I had to dye my blue hair brown to be professional.
> I want to wear my Jordans/Crocs.
> I try to be so serious all the time, and it's almost painful!

Reader, I want to fully invite you to give yourself permission to be yourself in ALL the ways you are you. To bring your blue hair, ripped jeans, sitting criss-cross applesauce, sarcastic, tattooed body, plant-loving, badass self into the counseling room. Please invite Peter Pan into the space and leave Peter Banning somewhere else. I give you permission to be your authentic self in and out of the counseling room.

Give Yourself Permission To Sit The Way You Sit

As you seek your most authentic self in the therapy room, I invite you to give yourself permission to chill out, relax, and get comfortable. New counselors get into a counseling room, tighten up, sit awkwardly, and get downright *weird*. Maybe your authentic self is weird (mine sure is). Then great! Be weird! But please do it relaxed. Sit comfortably in the chair. Put your legs where you want them; put your hands and arms where you want them. If it feels awkward, move and adjust. Use a pillow or not. Stop *pretending* to be a therapist and sit down in the chair, get comfortable, and just be you.

Sometimes, when I teach people how to do this (before they sit with actual clients), I invite them to sit on the floor, bring a rocking chair from the lobby area, sit criss-cross applesauce, bring a blanket, or put their feet up; you do you to get comfortable as you learn how to draw out your authentic self at first. Your most authentic self is much more accessible when you're a comfortable human in your own body in the counseling space.

Give Yourself Permission To Talk How You Talk

Use YOUR words. I encourage you to give yourself permission to use *your* words. The sassy words. The non-clinical words. The curse words. The I'm-not-trying-to-sound-smart words. Not the words that your professor uses that make them sound so clinical, profound, and smart. Use your version of those words. There are nine million ways to do counseling, and your way is the best way.

Let go of the words you think you're supposed to use, and just use the words that reflect your authentic self. I was watching a male student do a role-play where he was struggling to find his voice. He has a military background, tattoos over much of his body, and grew up with a dysfunctional, loving, serious f-bomb cursing family. When he tried to "act" like a therapist, it was awkward and incredibly inauthentic. When I asked him,

"Where did you go?" in reference to his personality that I had come to know and love, his colorful response indicated that he didn't know how to be himself and be clinical and "frilly." I invited him to think of integrating his authentic self like a pendulum. His pendulum had swung to the "frilly language" side. I gave him permission to let it swing to the "colorful language" side for a moment, try it out, and let it swing back and forth until he found a happy middle ground. And he did! He found a beautiful and authentic place that was true to him but also not filled with f-bombs or frilly, awkward, clinical language. Now, he's a brilliant clinician, working with clients from his true and authentic self.

Give Yourself Permission To Feel How You Feel

Please give yourself permission to *have emotions*, to listen to your emotions, trust your emotions, and bring them into the room. Lost? Say that! Confused? Say that! Struggling to keep up? Say that! Feeling sad about their story? Say that! I give you permission to have emotions and not be a robot. Your authentic emotions matter and are an important part of the therapeutic process. I had been working with a client for several months when she came into a session and shared the devastating news that she had experienced her fourth miscarriage. I felt so sad for her and with her. While she cried, I shared how my heart hurt for her, how devastating that news felt, and how it must have felt for her, too. My emotions helped me connect to hers. Listening to my own heart helped me connect to her heart. Your authentic self has emotions. Don't lock them up or keep them separate; *use* them to connect with others. *What you feel matters.*

> There are nine million ways to do counseling and your way is the best way.

During a supervision meeting, an intern brought in a video of a recent "disaster session," as she so lovingly called it. We sat and watched that video for forty minutes. My heart was racing, my armpits sweating. The new counselor had become triggered by the mom in a family session and didn't know what to do about it. She ended up handling the heated session well, but she wanted to learn how to use what she felt. She felt stuck between the adult children and the mom. She felt triggered by the mom's scolding of her children and of the counselor. She felt confused about why the mom kept changing the subject. So, she sat generally quiet in the session, aware of all of these feelings but not feeling confident about what she could bring into the room and not. I shared with her that it could be beneficial to *speak those feelings into the room.* She looked at me wide-eyed but willing. The next session, she did that very thing. The process and emotional expression were shared, and the family moved through something incredibly important that others also felt in the room but were too afraid to bring up. Sometimes, having emotions, naming those emotions, and carefully sharing them with our clients can be the best way through them.

Give Yourself Permission To Laugh

Reader, please *laugh.* I encourage you to give yourself permission to laugh, play, bring in humor, and have fun as a counselor. You are allowed to have fun and laugh. In fact, you are encouraged to. People need a balance of depth and lightness. Clients need light in the darkness, and we need to be able to model that for them and lead them there. I was working with a couple, and the man was sharing that it was exhausting for him to change to fit the needs of his wife. He brought up that it felt like Brendan Fraser in the movie *Bedazzled*[4] where the devil keeps telling him to be different versions of himself, and that's kind of what it felt like I was asking of him. I knew what he meant and I was tracking him, but in that moment, the first thing that came to me was, "I'm pretty sure what you're saying here is that I'm like the devil; did you just liken me to the devil?" We all laughed. A lot. And then I went back to address his genuine concern. But being real and true and witty is an important part of the process. Please find the balance of fun and laughter.

Give Yourself Permission To Be Creative

Try new things. Clients are all different and really deeply need your creativity. Please give yourself permission to get messy, take chances, make mistakes,[5] and be creative! So many of the greatest "interventions" I've ever done or heard others do came out of just making something up on the spot. Maybe it'll blow up in your face, or maybe it will work brilliantly! Either way, you'll learn.

A new intern was describing to me that she had an idea in the middle of her second-ever family therapy session. She gave each person a piece of paper and told them to write down a number indicating their level of connection as a family on a scale of one to ten. As they shared their numbers, the teen daughter, who had written a three, shared how her parents hadn't held something important she had shared with them very well, and it uncovered a beautiful conversation that lasted for several sessions after that. All because she followed a hunch to try some silly idea that came to her in the session. Take chances, use metaphors, think outside the box, make up interventions, and use your creative thoughts. And hear this: it's okay to make mistakes. I've made more mistakes in my career than many of you have even made attempts yet.

Clients Need You

Beautiful human, this world needs you. We need your authentic self. We need you to bring that authentic self into the counseling room. To connect with others, to model the importance of being honest with ourselves and others. We don't need some version of you pretending to be a therapist; we just need you. My hope is that this chapter has given you a permission slip to stop pretending to be a therapist. Stop putting on the cardigan, the fancy words, the sitting up straight with your coffee in your fancy mug, and just chill out. Relax. Laugh. Show them you care in ways that *you* are designed to care. Connect with clients in ways that feel true to you.

> Beautiful human, this world needs you.

Professor, writer, and theologian Henri Nouwen said, "One of the tragedies of our lives is that we keep forgetting who we are."[6] Even though I've invited you to give yourself permission slips, the reality is that it can feel like a battle between Peter Banning and Peter Pan. Sometimes, it's easy to forget who we are, especially as we learn new things and how to be in new spaces. The learning doesn't have to pull you into being Peter Banning. As you learn and grow, the great permission slip is that you never lose touch with the Peter Pan in you. The movie[2] ends like this: Peter Pan integrates his fun-loving, creative, silly self into his professional life. He doesn't change who he is. He integrates it. Reader, that is what I want you to give yourself permission to do. Stay Peter Pan, and bring that authentic part of you into this new space. It belongs there. It's part of you—a genuine and important part of you. My deep hope is that this chapter breathes life into you as a beautiful human who has so much to offer by just bringing your authentic self into the counseling room. Your clients need you, not some version of you. They need *you*.

CHAPTER SEVEN

Stay in Your Lane

T he student stood up in the middle of the role-play exercise, avoided eye contact, and bolted out the classroom door. The classroom hushed, and I could sense all eyes moving to me. The students were doing round-robin role-plays, where one student sits in the middle of the classroom with classmates circled around them, and another student in the middle acts as a client. After about three minutes of being the therapist, they swap out with another student therapist, and everyone gets a chance to swap in and out and practice a particular skill. Now that I write it out, it sounds like torture. Role-plays are bad enough, but doing it in front of the class sounds excruciating. There is a purpose, though. Trust me. And also, on behalf of all professors everywhere, I apologize for all the role-plays. We do them because they work. And they're awful. They can be both at the same time.

This particular student, who I knew pretty well, had just finished her role-play, stood up, and went straight out the door. I encouraged the class to continue as I traced her steps. I found her in an empty classroom nearby, pacing. She saw me walk in, and resting in our trusting relationship, she unleashed.

"Dr. Michelle, I SUCK!"

The shockwave of emotion in her voice broke the stillness of the room. Her words hung in the air for just a breath, and her body sensed the opposition of the silence of the classroom with the volume and intensity of her words. Turning down the volume and turning up the intensity of expression, she continued.

I'm not good at this!
I should quit.
Everyone else is better than me.
I'm a disaster in designer shoes.
I'm too old for this.

> Comparison is a tricky beast like that. We see things in others, and we are certain that not only do we not possess those skills, but we never, ever will.

The barrage of her reality cut through the space between us like a jagged knife. I gently asked her if I could interrupt her. I had a feeling the negative statements and feelings were pretty infinite, as was the desire to get them off her chest. Through this dance between anger and tears, she shared that everyone in the classroom was catching on to this particular skill except for her (which was definitely not my experience). She was certain she would never get the hang of it, would never pass the course, would definitely not graduate, and would never be able to get licensed. She was convinced she would never get and keep clients, they would all fire her immediately, and she would be the worst therapist in the history of therapists. She would stand by and watch all of her classmates passing her with ease, brilliance, and youthfulness—with little to no effort at all—and send her a friendly wave as they passed her by. Of course, this wasn't exactly true, but it sure felt that way to her. Comparison is a tricky beast like that. We see things in others, and we are certain that not only do we not possess those skills, but we never, ever will.

This student and I talked at length that afternoon about the importance of staying in her lane. In her "I'm worse than everyone" rant, she highlighted all the ways she would never be as skilled as me, how her classmates are far more brilliant than her, and she literally cursed those "master" videos[1] she had to watch in the theory class that made her feel even more unskilled and utterly incompetent. The comparison to everyone else around her and the unrealistic expectations of what it was like to be a beginner was a recipe for one big hot mess.

Learning To Drive

When you entered graduate school, you got on the on-ramp to the freeway as a learner. The same on-ramp that every single counselor before you has been on. Every single one of us. I traveled that on-ramp. And that's where many of you might be right now. Everything is new. Speeding up to the pace of the freeway feels a little (or a lot) scary, and you don't quite know how to use your blinker, stay between the lines, and check blind spots. Heck, the process of getting from the on-ramp to the freeway itself is terrifying.

It is terrifying for many, including me in the beginning. I had my hands on ten and two, my grip on the wheel was tight, and the need to pick up the pace to enter the freeway was so scary. I was scared about having the right paperwork. I was scared about inviting clients into the room. I was scared about writing my notes. I was scared about filling a 50-minute hour. I was scared about a lot of things in the beginning on the on-ramp.

But I figured it out. And you will, too—one breath and one mile at a time. Many of you, while doing your very best to stay in the lane you're in, watch the fast lane next to you. People driving in that fast lane are talking with their hands, changing lanes while checking blind spots, carrying on a conversation with ease, and even laughing and experiencing joy! And you want to be just like them. Not later, not in a year, *right now.*

You want it so desperately right now because being in the moment where this student burst out of the classroom feels like miles and miles away from where you want to be. You don't want to learn to crawl; you want to run. You're ready to go fast and don't want to start slow. It's excruciating to learn new words when you really just want to have a full conversation and read a whole book. You don't want to learn how to throw a football or do drills; you want to play a whole football game. I know. I really do. I see you. I see you with a deep desire to push the fast-forward button because being a beginner is really hard. Being a beginner is overwhelming, confusing, and scary. And the process of learning can feel long, tiresome, and lonely.

The tricky thing about being a beginner is that we look around at all those around us who are also beginners, and they sure don't feel like beginners to us. They feel like they're in a whole different lane, and we're all alone in our stupid beginner lane. Our head knows they are beginners, and we are able to rationalize that, but our hearts get it all scrambled up. It feels like we are the only ones not meeting the mark or learning the skill or mastering the concepts. We compare ourselves to others through these really distorted glasses where they are doing so much better than us in all the ways. And the feeling of loneliness turns to feeling inadequate, ill-equipped, and worthless. And you feel like maybe you should just quit.

For some of us, those distorted glasses were given to us directly by our ghosts. Damn it, there they are again, showing up where they aren't welcome. Those ghosts tell me, tell us, that it's not safe to be a learner or we aren't loved as much when we're still learning. Some of us were told to act more like our siblings or our best friend or the star player on the sports team. Push, learn, grow, strive, achieve. And those things are *good*, but not when compared to someone else. For some of us, unless we are performing at our best, we are subject to shame, rejection, disappointment, and loneliness. Mostly from ourselves.

Our Blind Spots

Many of us are really good at comparing ourselves to others in pretty destructive ways. My daughter's school recently offered students an opportunity to participate in a talent show. Completely optional. Many students signed up to dance, play an instrument, sing, draw, and show their silly and serious creative expressions with the school. My daughter decided to play a piano piece she had been working on not-so-religiously for a couple of months. She crammed the day before the performance and was ready to play it well enough.

As she started to play the song, a boy a year older than her a couple rows ahead of us turned to his mom, made a dramatic and exasperated face, and through forced whispers, shared with his mom, "That's the same song I'm working on." He didn't share it with excitement at the familiarity of it. He shared it with embarrassment and defeat. His shoulders slumped and his head slammed into his hands. As my daughter played the song, she tripped over notes, lost her place, and did the best she could without more practice. In all truthfulness, she played it just okay in terms of accuracy and skill. But what was so fascinating was the boy didn't notice her errors. He didn't notice she had played several wrong notes. He also didn't notice she lost her place and that the song wasn't played flawlessly. He was so caught up in feeling inadequate that he didn't notice the song he had just played was likely the same skill level as the one she was playing. In his head, he had already decided she was better, more skilled, more advanced, and moving along in the fast lane.

Reader, he was so worried about her showing up better than he could that he got lost in the comparison and didn't notice she is a beginner, too. And we do that, too. We get so caught up in how we aren't showing up or how we aren't measuring up; we lose sight of the skills we do have, the songs we do know how to play, or the struggles others also have. We don't notice them struggling or losing their place. And we surely don't realize when we see that gift or skill in someone else that *they see the same thing*. They look at us without us knowing and compare themselves to us. We just never know about that side of the coin.

Sometimes, the other side of that coin is that when we're in the slow lane, we want to be in the fast lane, and when we're in the fast lane, we want to be in a faster lane. Comparison is tricky like that, too. We forget we used to be a learner and aren't anymore, but there are still others in faster lanes. In two of the courses I teach, I invite "mentors" to help with the class. These mentors are students in the program who have already taken these specific courses and have progressed to internships. When I meet with them before the class, many of them express they haven't learned enough to mentor anybody. They so easily forget that while they are still beginners, they have learned a great deal already. They are not in the same beginner lane they used to be in. They learned so many things in that first beginner lane and have merged into another lane that can also feel like being a beginner.

Every Lane Feels So Slow

It's often so easy to forget where we were when we started. It is easy to lose touch with the idea that when we started, we thought the purpose of counseling was to fix people. To fix up all the problems and put a nice little bow on top. We forget that when we started, we had no clue how to start a session, or introduce ourselves, or ask clients a direct question. And if you don't know how to do those things, it's okay; you'll learn. It's okay to be right where you are. Being a beginner is okay. It does not define your worth. You are growing. Over time, we learn how to call a client's parent, and how to ask for custody paperwork, and how to ask about suicidal ideation, and how to manage more than one person in the room. All of those lanes have new and scary things at first. And then after a while, they're not new anymore, but we replace them with more new things so it still feels like we're beginners. The amount of new things to learn doesn't stop. Once you are no longer a beginner, the comparison still follows us around if we let it. It doesn't go away because there are always faster lanes. Always.

While it may have been several years since I wanted to jump out of my counselor beginner lane into the fast lane, whenever we learn new skills, we have to learn to stay in our lane. We can't jump from the on-ramp to the fast lane. It's dangerous for us, it's dangerous for others, and driving (and learning!) just doesn't work that way. When I started writing this book, my desire to start in the fast lane was incredibly strong and overwhelming. I didn't want to start in the beginner lane, and I sure didn't (don't) want to stay there. See, I even want to use past tense there, but it's really still present tense. I'm in the slow lane. I don't want to learn how to drive first and use the blinker. I want to set my cruise control in that fast lane and laugh and converse and talk with my hands.

Those people in the fast lane over there make it look so easy. I want to be like and write like all the others that went before me and inspired me. I want to be vulnerable like Brene Brown.[2] I want to be brilliant like Aundi Kobler.[3] I want to be authentic like Emily Freeman.[4] I want to be creative like Hannah Brencher.[5] And I want it *now*. But learning isn't like that. Being a beginner is all about learning how to stay in your lane and having realistic expectations of what driving in that lane is like. And it sucks. It doesn't mean *I* suck, but it sure sucks—just like that student declared. Learning is hard, especially when we have such amazing examples all around us of the brilliance of where our learning leads us. Eventually.

Own Your Lane

During her last year of graduate school, I talked a lot with the student who burst out of the classroom about the dangers of comparison. She, like many beginners in anything, felt insecure and constantly compared herself to others. She wanted so desperately to jump into the fast lane. Over time, this student began to realize that while staying in your lane is difficult, it's also incredibly important. My hope for her to stay in her lane transformed into her own mantra, her own hope. She began living by her own mantra in her work to fight the gravity pull of comparison. She adopted, "I haven't missed out on what's for me." A personal mantra that builds a strong shield inside of her and deflects the attempts of comparison to work its way into her spirit. It reminds her not to give up. This phrase is an important reminder for her that those passing her by in the fast lane *aren't taking anything away from her.*

> Your progress is your progress and is not to be measured against anyone else's actual or perceived progress. It is what it is. You are who you are, and that is enough.

We all have gifts that are so brilliantly unique to us. To you. You have those, reader. Each and every one of you. Yes, you, there, who thinks I'm talking to everyone but you. You, too. You have unique gifts and skills there in your beginner lane that I don't have over here in my lane. That no amount of practice or theory will gift to me. The brilliance of your unique self is a gift—because it's yours! It's yours to have and yours to share with others in the process of counseling. Your brilliance is already in the lane with you. You don't have to merge into another lane to find it. It's right there, already trucking along inside you.

You're Not Driving Alone

The brilliance of our unique selves can sometimes be discovered in the close cousin of comparison in places of inspiration. When we can watch others demonstrate their authentic expression of self, it can give us permission to do the same. In my graduate program, while watching those amazing and incredibly old and dated "masters" videos, we were tasked with making a list of phrases, characteristics, and authentic expressions that we found inspiring in those masters. We were encouraged not to compare ourselves to them or try to imitate them but to invite them to inspire us. I will never be as quirky and crazy as Carl Whitaker, but I do love that he gave me permission to bring quirky and crazy into sessions. I watched in awe as he was unapologetically authentic in his presence and interactions when he did his work. He inspired me to be fully and authentically me in the counseling space. And watching Sue Johnson inspired me to be direct, curious, and share my places of attunement with my clients. Watching Virginia Satir gave me the permission slip to be creative, to make stuff up right on the spot, and to bring a little play into the session. Sure, it took me a long time to actually put all that into practice, but it helped me realize that inspiration is there, right alongside comparison, no matter what lane you're in.

During the last day of one of my intensive clinical courses that involves three full eight-hour days of role-plays with one another, I asked the students to put everything away on their desks. Pack up their papers and computers and distractions. I asked them to put away the pressure to learn and take notes and show up in a particular, expected, academic way. Then, I wrote a prompt at the top of the whiteboard that simply said, "Places I feel growth." I encouraged them, when they felt inspired, to come up and share. And I waited. The quiet room shifted into a space of contemplation. Of reflection. Of *self*-reflection. How have I grown? In my own lane, at my own pace, how have I grown this semester? Soon, they began to write. And what happened surprised me. After several unique responses, students began placing check marks after the things they also experienced. And soon, there was a list of 8-10 reflections and

10-12 check marks after each of them.

Letting go of perfectionism ✓✓✓✓✓✓✓✓✓
Being curious ✓✓✓✓✓
Growth mindset ✓✓✓✓✓✓✓
Accepting of self ✓✓✓✓✓✓✓✓✓✓✓
It's okay to make mistakes ✓✓✓✓✓✓✓

And there's one last one. As I sat there, still quiet at the back of the classroom, I watched as *every single student* added a checkmark to:

It's okay to be a beginner ✓✓✓✓✓✓✓✓✓✓✓✓✓✓✓✓✓✓ ✓✓✓✓

Twenty-two check marks. Every single student decided it was okay to be a beginner. They realized being on the on-ramp or in the slow lane was right where they needed to be. In that moment, I didn't care if they learned the perfect intervention, how to apply all the theories, or when to interrupt. What flooded my heart was that these students learned from one another in that moment that they were all in it together. Beginners encouraging beginners. Seeing beginners as brilliant. They all felt like beginners and realized it was okay.

The last student to place their check mark chuckled, saying, "I think I'm the last one," and the class joined in conversation while I remained quiet in the back. They shared stories about how they thought they were the only one who felt like a beginner. They shared phrases that communicated, "It's crazy to know we were all in it together," and "I had no idea, I thought it was just me that felt lost and overwhelmed," and "Feeling together in it feels so different today than it did at the beginning," and

"I wish I had known this the first day." Reader, the beginners wished they had known in the important parts of their hearts that everyone felt like a beginner on the first day. They wished they had spoken these words to one another. The words that said I see you, and you are amazing. "I'm learning so much from you. You inspire me." To battle the ghosts that told them to compare. To judge. To evaluate. To feel smaller than. And listen to the angels invite you into the space of inspiration and encourage you to share with one another, "You inspire me." Yes, you, on that on-ramp or beginner lane—you inspire me. You inspire your fellow colleagues, and you inspire me.

As the students continued, they shared how hard it was to do the role-plays after someone else because they all felt the person before them was far more brilliant than they could ever be. This classroom of students spent over thirty minutes sharing with one another about comparison. They used words like "the actual worst thing," and "so hard," and "comparison trap." They shared how much it sucks when you're trying to learn something, and someone does it and makes it look so easy. They began speaking directly to one another, saying phrases like, "I thought the exact same thing about you!" And around and around they went. Each of them shared the brilliance that another classmate had and how they wished they could see that in themselves.

In that discussion, they were reminded that we are all brilliant in our own unique ways, which elicited comparison and inspiration from others. They shared how silly it felt, now that they were talking about it, to try to be like those master theorists or to be like their professor who had been doing counseling for twenty years. These students, unknown to them (which I did share with them later), inspired me. That's right—in their on-ramp, beginner lane, they gave me ideas and inspired me in my lane. Because that's how learning can work if we step out of comparison. No matter the lane we're in, there's always learning for us.

As these students in the classroom shared back and forth, I found great power in students talking directly to one another, giving each other encouragement and inspiration right there in their lane. And I want that for you, too, reader. I want someone to tell you that you are amazing and brilliant in your lane, on the on-ramp, or thinking about driving onto the on-ramp. I want your heart people to show up for you and tell you that you are worthy right smack dab where you currently stand. In that lane right there. Sure, you'll be brilliant in the next lane, too, but you are so brilliant right there in the lane you're in. Your progress is your progress and is not to be measured against anyone else's actual or perceived progress. It is what it is. You are who you are, and that is enough. You are enough. Not later, not in a year, right now. You have unique value right where you are—right now. In that lane or the next lane or on the on-ramp. Not some day. Right now.

CHAPTER EIGHT

Sacred Air

A few days ago my phone rang, and I looked over and saw that a colleague of mine was calling. When she reaches out, she usually texts me, so a phone call was a bit unusual. Wondering if something was wrong, I answered. There was silence on the other end, followed by quiet sounds of crying. She quickly said, "I'm okay. Everything is okay, but as soon as I called you, the tears came."

This colleague and I have been through some things together. We've grown together, cried together, and encouraged one another in clinical growth edges. On the other end of the phone from her tears, I softly spoke her name and let her tears continue to fall. Soon, she shared a struggle she was having with a client that triggered something quite painful from her personal areas of growth. She and I have talked about this struggle several times over the years, through tears of pain and tears of self-awareness. She has processed so much with her own counselor to move through this growth edge, and over time, it has become less of a roadblock for her.

However, it never goes away, and sometimes that ghost is a little louder than she and I would prefer it to be. She felt sad, overwhelmed, disappointed, and insecure. She and I both knew there were no words of wisdom here. She knows the work, and I know the work. She didn't need me to give her advice. She didn't need me to tell her she needed to do more work in this area. She didn't need me to sugarcoat it for her, either. She didn't need me to fill this tender space with words or solutions. In not so many words, it just sucked. And we were in the suck together. She needed me to be in it with her. She needed to sit with me, and have me honor this space for her, and just be with her. Simply and solely.

This silent dialogue reminds me of a famous quote from the beloved Winnie the Pooh.[1]

"Today was a Difficult Day," said Pooh.
There was a pause.
"Do you want to talk about it?" asked Piglet.
"No," said Pooh after a bit. "No, I don't think I do."
"That's okay," said Piglet, and he came and sat beside his friend.
"What are you doing?" asked Pooh.
"Nothing, really," said Piglet. "Only, I know what Difficult Days are like. I quite often don't feel like talking about it on my Difficult Days either.
"But goodness," continued Piglet, "Difficult Days are so much easier when you know you've got someone there for you. And I'll always be here for you, Pooh."

And as Pooh sat there, working through in his head his Difficult Day, while the solid, reliable Piglet sat next to him quietly, swinging his little legs...he thought that his best friend had never been more right."

And, dear reader, your presence for others in the counseling space is often the most important healing space you can create. The sacredness of your presence communicates, "I'm with you." There can be so much comfort, healing, and holding in togetherness. No necessary movement or solutions, simply being present with another. With this colleague, I held space for her. She called for silent comfort, for holding by a knowing other, and for nothing more than to be in sadness with another human. Nothing more and nothing less.

But as counselors, we often feel like more is needed. And so we try so hard. In our deep desire to help, we get sucked into the trap of movement.

We try so desperately to
fix
solve
move
act
help
do
talk
find the solution
We just keep trying *so hard.*

This healing space, though, this sacred air, requires us to let go, rather than to work harder. Clients often come to our spaces because others in their lives have not been with them in ways that have been helpful, safe, and nurturing. They often yearn for us and others to hold them (figuratively) and to attend to their needs and longings. But because of their ghosts and the noise of life that surrounds us all, they often don't know how to identify and ask for those needs to be fulfilled. Just like you and me, our clients often don't know how to ask for these needs, don't know how to reach for others, and don't know how to express the longing to be seen and felt; *to be joined*.

And what I've learned over time is that sometimes some of the most important healing in counseling

Isn't an action, it's a lack of action.
Isn't words, it's the absence of words.
Isn't solutions, it's the feelings that come with being stuck.
Isn't movement, it's stability.
Isn't fixing, it's being together.

Sometimes what is needed is togetherness, stability, emotions, and stillness. The whispers that say to our hearts "Just sit here a while with me and just be". Our bodies need this stillness, this softening. And clients need this too. They need us to create a space for them to quiet the noise, to give them space and stillness. Where we can just be, as we are, who we are. Because it's in this stillness where they find themselves. This stillness is where they find their emotions, their tenderness, and their needs. This stillness that we create with them allows them to slow and soften. And it's these spaces, between, that create a sacred with-ness.

Trying Softer

These moments are not created by doing more and trying harder. These moments of safe and calming presence are created by us *trying softer*[2]. To just *be*. To trust that who you are in the room with the client is enough. And sometimes, your presence is all the client needs. Trying softer means letting go of the desire for movement or talking. It's trusting that when silence creates stillness, that is so fully enough.

And the truth is, when we try softer, the small things like stillness, presence, and quiet can bring forth the most important parts of the healing process. The release of the need to try harder brings a softening of our grip to move, change, and heal and allows for that space, that air, to enter the therapy room and fill the space between us with healing.

The space, the stillness, between client and counselor is sometimes present in unexpected places. The other day, I walked into my internship classroom, ready to watch a student video from their internship site and discuss case conceptualization. As I settled in, the student presenting that day was in the classroom, getting his computer setup to show his work with his client on the screen. He let out a big sigh and flopped the case formulation in front of me. He shared he felt nervous about his presentation and client video because he did not feel he was doing good work. He shared he tried so hard to help this client but felt like his efforts weren't enough. He felt the session was a disaster, didn't feel proud of his work, and felt vulnerable and exposed.

As the class began, we sat together, the small group of students and I, and silently watched this clinician-in-training share his therapy session with us. As I watched this video, I saw a seventeen-year-old client struggling in many aspects of their life, including questions about their identity. They lost friends in the process. Their parents had essentially stopped talking to them even though they lived in the same home. They were struggling in school and didn't feel like they knew what was next in their life. The client was confused, overwhelmed, disappointed, sad, and lonely. Everyone who had been there for them before was gone.

As the client shared these experiences the therapist was gently leaning in, his eyes communicated sadness as he listened to the story pouring out from his client. Even through the screen, I could sense the power of his presence with this client. His minimal words were offered slowly and softly. There were no questions, no directing the conversation, and no desire to act, move, fix, solve, or help. His *presence* communicated "This space right here is what's important".

As the client shared these experiences, stories, and emotions, the therapist sat quietly, occasionally offering a statement of empathy or reflection. "Wow, that sounds like a lot", "How is that for you?", "Uh-huh", "That's tricky", and so on. And the client talked. And cried. And expressed anger, fear and regret and sadness. He sat gently in those spaces and emotions with the client. He didn't worry about interventions or reflections. The therapist was present—purely and solely present. The air between them didn't communicate stagnancy, lack of progress, or awkwardness, it suggested *holding and tenderness*. The therapist created a sacred space.

And in that moment, in that space with that client, that is exactly what the client needed. They needed to feel this therapist was a witness to their pain and suffering. They needed the space to explore what they were feeling because they didn't have anyone else to do that with them. And it was beautiful and the deep and good work of a counselor.

> My deep wish for us counselors is that we can redefine what good clinical work looks like. Sometimes, good clinical work is theory and interventions, and other times, it offers simple and pure sacred air that only slow, silent, still, with-ness can communicate.

I turned to the therapist, asked him to pause the video of his clinical work, and smiled tenderly at him. "Mark," I said gently, "this is beautiful." He looked up at me from under the bill of his cap where he had been hiding and said, "*Really*?!" He shared he was feeling this tension between "I didn't do enough" and "Everything I did was exactly enough". For him, there was such pressure to be working harder, doing more, being more active; and watching his work on video and having others watch it in this academic space made him feel like he wasn't *doing* enough. He feared his skills were not enough. The self-imposed expectation of the work of a counselor prevented him from placing value on his presence. His fears minimized the with-ness that happened in the sacred space between the client and the therapist that he had felt when he was in the moment. It made him think that his with-ness wasn't clinical work. My deep wish for us counselors is that we can redefine what good clinical work looks like. Sometimes, good clinical work is theory and interventions, and other times, it's the sacredness of stillness that brings all the healing needed. The actual healing process was in the sacred air of the quiet, together, silence. And it was not only enough, it was everything.

Coming Alongside

These spaces of stillness and quiet are not nurtured in many relationships, though. We don't learn that trying softer can be where the hard work happens. This sacred stillness is the space between you and your client, between you and me, right now reader. I invite you to take a deep breath and call on a memory and the feelings where you felt so *with* another person and it didn't require words or movement. The space where it's not silence, but it's *stillness* because in stillness you are with another; it's relational.

I invite you to imagine the subtle differences between silence and stillness. I invite you to think of stillness as coming alongside. How might our work with clients be different if we embodied the togetherness and the coming alongside like Piglet did with Pooh, rather than a transactional set of back-and-forth communication? This with-ness, of sitting beside, of joining, creates a stillness and a sacredness that shifts in my heart. While we may not actually move our chairs to be side by side with our clients, how can we express this level of "I'm here with you" that only a lack of words, a sacred air can communicate?

> The actual healing process was in the sacred air of the quiet, together, silence. And it was not only enough, it was everything.

Sacred air is the healing presence of *you* in the room with clients. It's the space between two humans that sometimes is just perfectly enough. It's a silent presence that can sometimes communicate more than words can. Sacred air is stillness. Space. Holding. Slowing. And being truly and solely present with a client.

Rest in the stillness of the therapy room
and believe that sometimes
It is enough.
The holding you are doing
your still presence
with your client
here in this stillness

is so powerful and completely enough.
The stillness is communicating everything that words could communicate
but differently
deeper
more profoundly.
Your mere existence with another in their pain and healing
creates the healing space
that is the sacred air,
the giving and receiving
the with-ness
the co-creation of a shifting narrative.
Healing is happening in these deep and quiet spaces
where breath lives
where tears are seen
where the deep sacredness of togetherness
speaks all that needs to be spoken.
Where the tenderness and power of your presence
delivered with no words at all
is everything.

As counselors, your presence matters. Side by side, heart to heart, just the experience of *with-ness.* With-ness of being together, in a space, with another human, right in the middle of the mess they're going through. That with-ness is sacred space. Like the wisdom of Piglet, our aloneness doesn't feel so isolating when you're in it with another. "Difficult Days are so much easier when you know you've got someone there for you." And that, counselor, is you.

CHAPTER NINE

You First

I was standing by, watching a live role-play with a student who wanted to go "deeper" with the client she had been role-playing with for a few weeks. The student therapist felt stuck trying to encourage the client to find deeper emotions and reflections and would often go back to surface-level problem solving. At one particular point in the role-play, the fellow-student-turned-client was sharing how her parents just didn't understand how much she loved her high school boyfriend and would miss him deeply when the family moved out of state. She felt frustrated by the situation. The therapist quickly moved to problem solving and away from her own stated goal of going deeper into process and emotions.

I gently interrupted and encouraged the therapist to move into exploring what the client meant when she shared she felt "frustrated." As much as the therapist tried to connect with the client's frustration, she couldn't quite attune to the client's experience. I then shifted the focus from the client's experience to the therapist's experience and encouraged the student to sink into her own body and reflect on what she was feeling in that particular moment, to feel what was coming up inside of *her*. She turned and stared at me briefly and shared that she wasn't sure. She shared that she, too, felt frustrated but wasn't able to expand on that or attune to her own thoughts and feelings in the present moment. She couldn't quite identify anything deeper than frustration and couldn't articulate exactly what she felt frustrated about, other than the role-play wasn't going well, and she was frustrated she couldn't bring the client deeper.

> A therapist can't walk clients to a deeper, more authentic, attuned place without first doing the same for themselves.

This is a common experience for new therapists. Beginning therapists often assume their role in counseling is to help people by giving advice and fixing their problems. And while symptom reduction is often a part of the counseling process, therapy is a much more relational, integrative process that involves relationship with and modeling from the therapist. It's a symbiotic process. A therapist can't walk clients to a deeper, more authentic, attuned place without first doing the same for themselves.

One of the most important aspects of becoming an effective therapist is also one of the most overlooked: ourselves. Most of us, clients and therapists alike, go through our entire day without really ever stopping to process how we feel about anything beyond a surface level. We simply skip the self-attunement part, both outside and inside the therapy space. And as therapists, this part of learning about *ourselves* is a crucial part of learning about others. As a therapist, you are part of the system of change, and if you yourself cannot attune to your own needs, feelings, and longings, it will be very difficult—perhaps even impossible—for you to do this with others. And, my dear reader, you are worth this work. The depths of you are worth getting to know intimately.

You Can't Fake It Forever

Sometimes, we think we can trick the process, outsmart ourselves and our ability to attune to others. Sometimes, we think, "I can work hard to be attuned with my *clients* without being attuned with *myself*." Sorry to burst your delusional bubble, reader: you can't. Without being present with yourself in your own mind, in your own heart, having awareness of your current experiences, you cannot fully be with another. But we try all the time. And in some ways, we can fake it really well. We can learn the words to say and the phrases to use to fake attunement with self and others. But when the deep work of therapists is required, going "deeper" cannot be done without doing the work ourselves and going deeper within. The student therapist in the role-play really hoped and believed she could go deeper with the client without being able to go deeper with herself. But it just doesn't work that way. Self-attunement is an essential prerequisite to being attuned to others. You have to start with you.

The reality is that there are a lot of really good reasons why we get stuck and cannot attune to ourselves. And a lot of those reasons have to do with our ghosts. I'm so sorry that's the case. If you're anything like this student, I can feel your deep longing to connect with that inner part of you. I can feel you wondering if that part of you even exists, fearing it might not. I know that your experiences, your traumas from your distant past, and maybe even ones not so long ago, tell you to act a certain way, talk a certain way, and *be* a certain way. And, in doing that, you start abandoning your own thoughts, feelings, and attunement to yourself. You start believing others know better for you than you do for yourself. You're disconnected, disassociated, or disembodied from yourself, or all of the above. Many of us have literally become conditioned to *not* listen to our bodies, to not sense, intuit, or feel anything our bodies or our hearts are telling us. And we simply stop listening.

Reader, this is important work for you as a therapist. You cannot ignore your ability to attune to yourself and be an effective therapist and attune to others. You have to develop self-awareness so that you know how your responses or reactions might help or harm clients in the therapeutic process. Developing self-awareness and becoming attuned to our own experience allows us to understand and accept our own feelings, thoughts, and behaviors and to respond to them in a healthy way, for both us and our clients.

For many of us humans and counselors, it takes a great deal of practice. For many of us, it starts by becoming attuned to what's going on inside of us, around us, and with people we've interacted with. The first part of developing this self-attunement is becoming aware of what's coming up for us in one particular moment in time. Right here and right now.

There is a scene in Harry Potter[1] where Dumbledore, the wizard headmaster, puts his wand to his head and pulls out, like a magic thread, one thought, isolating it from the rest. He places it in a large magic bowl called the Pensieve. He says, "One simply siphons the excess thoughts from one's mind, pours them into the basin, and examines them at one's leisure. It becomes easier to spot patterns and links, you understand, when they are in this form." This is much like the process of becoming attuned and self-aware. It involves taking a look at all the things we may be feeling and examining them a little bit more, one at a time, with intention and care. Focusing on one part of our emotional experience and attuning to it allows us to be more tender and aware of what each of those pieces or threads is all about. Honoring each of them is important and a crucial part of becoming more self-attuned.

What Are You Feeling Right Now?

Learning how to pull one out at a time takes practice. A few years ago, I invited a licensed clinician to join the class I was teaching and do a role-play demonstrating a particular theory. He was sitting at the front of the room of students with two empty chairs awaiting his clients. He shared he was feeling a bit overwhelmed. I asked him to identify, in front of the class, what he was attuning to in his body and in his heart, what he was experiencing *here* and *now*.

The room went quiet, and he took a deep breath. He closed his eyes, tilted his head upwards, and took a deep, cleansing breath. It's almost as if we could see him sinking into himself, into his core experience, into his heart. We could see him shuttle from his head thinking space to his heart feeling space.

After a full minute, with his eyes still shut and his head still lifted upwards, he slowly shared that he could feel heat in his body, indicating he was nervous. He shared he could feel his head wanting to fill with tasks and interventions; he could feel his heart wanting to really stay present with the clients, tracking them from not only their words but the meaning behind the words. He shared he felt excitement and energy in the room, possibly contributing to his nervousness or his desire to show up well.

He shared, his voice filling with emotion, that he also felt tired. As we watched him share this, we saw him shuttle into his heart even further. He swallowed. His cheeks flushed. Fighting away the tears, he shared that another part of what he felt was sadness for his wife and a struggle she was battling. He also identified that when he listens to his heart, he feels incredible insecurity. He shared he doubts his ability to show up in the ways he wants to do. He further identified that he feels a deep desire for learning and connecting with others. And an important part of what came up for him was the feeling of support, love, and camaraderie with those watching his process. He shared that he felt love, compassion, and warmth from others.

> Being attuned to yourself is a prerequisite for being attuned to someone else.

Friends, we learned so much more about the heart of counseling through his deep sense of attuning to himself than we ever could from his counseling demonstration. In identifying his own feelings in the present moment when he was able to attune to himself, he was able to identify, like the Pensieve, his present process and experience. He attuned to each part, each thread of an experience or emotion, one at a time, with tenderness and love—not judgment. He didn't seek to explain or justify or make himself feel "better" about each of those things. It was the process of self-attunement. In identifying his own experiences and feelings in that space, he was also connecting it to how it would help him be with his clients, and that is the foundation for learning and building intuition and attunement.

Being attuned to oneself in the current moment is the first crucial part of learning to be attuned to another human. Being attuned *to yourself* is a prerequisite for being attuned to someone else. And being attuned isn't about fixing the things we discover when we attune to ourselves. When you tune into yourself, you are recognizing it, sitting with it. You're bringing to the surface what can be pushed, shoved, and hidden underneath, often in an attempt to pretend to move on from it. But when we become aware of all that's coming up inside of us, two important things can happen. First, our awareness helps us recognize how it might interact with our ability to be with another. And second, when we sink into the entirety of what's coming up for us, we can more powerfully love all of those parts in ourselves. And we practice sitting in those spaces with all the parts of ourselves so we can sit with all of those parts in our clients as well. Like the therapist who couldn't quite bring her clients "deeper," she first needed to know what "deeper" was like for herself and how it felt to be there in her body and in her heart.

Running Into "That" Friend

As we learn how to attune to ourselves, sometimes it can feel like unexpectedly running into "that" friend—the friend who has a deep sense of knowing. When they look at you, they really look at you and see all the places of pain and insecurity. You know the one. The friend who knows when you're lying when you say you're "fine." Sometimes, I avoid being present with myself so I can avoid being "that" friend for myself, the one who uncovers the painful places, holds up the mirror, and gives me insight that is needed but easily avoided. But I want you to be that friend for yourself who asks, "How are you doing, really?" and means it. I want you to ask yourself how you are, be curious, and listen to the response.

This is exactly what this therapist did prior to the role-play demonstration. He silently attuned to himself and everything that was coming up when he listened, and then shared it. I want you to be that person for you, one who asks how you are and really listens. And if you've ever had that friend in your life, they don't solve or fix; they listen with deep compassion, and they invite you into sacred air in the process of attuning to yourself.

When I can listen to all the things coming up for myself, I can begin to sort through them one at a time and honor all the feelings that come up, like Dumbledore and the Pensieve. This process of pulling out one thought or experience I'm having in the here and now, this self-attunement can help me begin to go deeper into what might be all mixed up in one ball. Like the example above, the therapist initially said he was feeling "overwhelmed," but when he was invited to self-attune to what "overwhelmed" was really all about, many different emotions and experiences came up for him. And acknowledging all of these is a necessary part of our work to help others go "deeper" and help ourselves do the same thing. When I can attune to my own emotions and experiences, I can be more kind and loving to myself. And, it helps me separate what thoughts and emotions are mine from which ones are my clients. While this helps avoid countertransference, it is much more about your own process. It's an honoring of you, your needs, your pains, your joys, and how they settle into the depths of you and how you, in turn, are able to be with your clients.

Slice It Thinner

The other day, I was getting ready to go into a session I had been dreading all week. I sat in my chair for the few moments I had before inviting the clients in and shut my eyes, took a slow, deep breath, and silently asked myself, "What's coming up for me?" My first and easiest response was, "I feel anxious." I could have stopped there. I was feeling anxious. I could say, "I attuned to myself, and I feel anxious." But what we learn over time about feelings and emotions is that sometimes, they can all lump together into one, and what we label as "anxious" or "scared" or "angry" is really a lot of other things. When I was learning about emotions and self-attunement a few years ago, a mentor asked me to "slice it thinner," meaning, what else is a part of that "anxiety" I was feeling? So before that session, I was able to begin slicing "anxious" thinner and thinner into the specific parts that made up this particular kind of anxious. That day, when I began to slice "anxious" thinner, I came up with:

I feel insecure.

The greater feeling of "anxiety," when I sliced it thinner, included insecurity. And identifying that part of my anxiety was incredibly important. Insecurity settles into my heart in different places than anxiety does. I have tenderness towards insecurity that I don't have towards anxiety.

And when I sliced insecure even thinner, I came up with:

I feel insecure when this client challenges me. Her challenges make me question my knowledge—and for me, knowledge is so tightly connected to worth. My insecurity here, sliced thinner, leads me to feel unworthy. And you know what? I am quite familiar with this ghost and how to love those parts of me well.

And if I go back to the original feeling of anxiety, I can ask myself, "What else is the anxiety about?" I can slice that thinner again and look for the other parts that are also in there alongside "insecure" and "unworthy." And when I do, I find I feel overwhelmed by my client load that day. I discover I'm also preoccupied and eager to hear about my daughter's day because she is going to be brave and have an important conversation with a teacher today. And if I keep slicing my anxiety thinner yet, I find other things that are so important for me to know about myself. Pulling these pieces out one at a time and taking a look at each of them helps me develop compassion and respond to myself in more loving and kind ways than I might have if I stayed on the surface of "anxious." It helped me go deeper into honest, tender, and more vulnerable places of myself.

What about the therapist-student who struggled to identify the deeper parts of "frustrated?" Well, she's in the middle of doing this work with me, her supervisors, her mentors, and her therapist. She is beginning to see that her feelings matter. She's starting to learn she's had a long history of avoiding what's coming up for her because it has never served her well. She was in environments (home, work, marriage) that ignored or minimized her feelings and what was coming up for her, so she did, too. But now she's starting to be able to slice "frustrated" thinner and discover that within it, there's insecurity, imposter syndrome, and embarrassment. She was able to discover she has a deep desire to figure this out for herself and her clients.

You are such a crucial part of the change process, reader. The feelings you have matter. The events going on in your life outside the counseling room matter; they impact you, and that's okay! When you can identify what's coming up for you, you can become familiar with the depths of emotion, the depths of humanity, and the depths of pain and suffering. And once you've traveled there with yourself, you can bring clients to the deeper place of health and healing. Until you attune to yourself, you'll have a hard time attuning to the deep needs of other people. Likewise, when you can attune to yourself, you'll experience a symphony of sounds that will help you connect with others. And this attunement to self and others creates beautiful, therapeutic music that is the heart of the work of a counselor.

CHAPTER TEN

Follow the Flight of Song

"We cannot see our reflection in running water. It is only in still water that we can see."[1]

Taoist Proverb

W hen I was growing up, my dad would recite poetry. He'd sing it, speak it, and play it on the piano or with one of his several harmonicas. We didn't have magazines in the bathroom; we had poetry books. One of the poems I learned by heart when I was young is "The Arrow and the Song" by Henry Wadsworth Longfellow. It goes like this:

"The Arrow and the Song"[2]
By Henry Wadsworth Longfellow

I shot an arrow into the air,
It fell to earth, I knew not where;
For, so swiftly it flew, the sight
Could not follow it in its flight.

I breathed a song into the air,
It fell to earth, I knew not where;
For who has sight so keen and strong,
That it can follow the flight of song?

Long, long afterward, in an oak
I found the arrow, still unbroke;
And the song, from beginning to end,
I found again in the heart of a friend.

The good work of a counselor is found here in the second stanza of this poem. How does a counselor listen in ways that they can follow the flight of song? I invite you to read it again and then close your eyes. Feel for a moment what it might be like to notice the flight of a song. Not hearing the words of the song, but noticing the flight of it. Noticing the nuances, and the song dancing in the breeze, and the twists and the turns it makes. Like a leaf blowing from the origin of its branch, it floats and twirls in the wind before it meets the earthly tones of words. If we listen to the song, we hear the words, and it becomes easy to listen only to the content of the song. However, if we follow the flight of it, those with sight so keen and strong can attune to the flight. This is listening with the ear of our hearts. This is attunement.

Attunement is the process of listening and noticing with a deep and engaged sense of self and others. Attunement is being aware of what clients (and ourselves) are *not* saying, noticing it, feeling it, and sensing it (although their words are important, too). Clients can unintentionally trick us so easily into believing their words are the most important part of what they say. But the truth is, they often communicate the most important things in ways that have absolutely nothing to do with the words they speak. Actually, you and I do this, too. The words you and I say can be a complete and utter distraction to what we really want to say. Sometimes, what people and clients share is "noise." Sorry, but it's true. We all, us and clients alike, cover our true feelings with explanations, justifications, fear-based, pride-protecting, emotion-covering noise.

As much as I would love to tell you that I don't do this, that I communicate directly and share my most true emotions with others all the time, that simply isn't true. And my husband and tween daughter know this. They have learned to attune to me most of the time (and me to them) and can read what lies underneath my words. Sometimes, when I say I'm "fine," my daughter looks at me, gives me a once-over, gives me this stink-eye-smirk as only she can do, and says, "I think you need a hug," and wraps her sweet arms around me and leans her whole body into mine.

She knows, through her attunement to my body, my with-drawnness, my less-than-spunky mood, and *not* through my words, that I'm not really that "fine" at all. And do you know what attunement does for me? For us? It softens us. It softens clients. It makes me feel seen and makes me want to lean in. My sweet daughter, cutting through the stoic "I'm fine," melts me into a puddle of tears that allows me to put congruent words to my tears through attunement. My sweet daughter followed the flight of the song and found it smack dab in the middle of our hug. Speaking directly to what my heart needed, not what my words shared. If my sweet daughter had chosen not to attune, or missed it altogether, I would have remained alone in my process, bottled up, closed off from the realities of my loneliness and disappointment.

And this happens with all of us so much of the time. We need people to see us. It's really that simple and that complex.

We need people to attune to us, to reach for us, and to follow the flight of song amid our words to our hearts.

> If we listen to the song, we hear the words, and it becomes easy to listen only to the content of the song. However, if we follow the flight of it, those with sight so keen and strong can attune to the flight. This is listening with the ear of our hearts. This is attunement.

Underneath The Noise

The true art of listening is hearing what is spoken underneath what we are really saying. Attunement is noticing the pieces hidden below the surface and speaking into them, reaching for them, and hugging them. Thirteenth-century poet Rumi wrote, "There is a voice that doesn't use words. Listen."[3] And I think he was talking about attunement. That is what my daughter did for me and what we can do for our clients (minus the warm hug part). Attunement is both a self-attunement and an other-attunement. When we attune to ourselves, we sink into our hearts and our bodies and identify what we are feeling. The self-attunement highlighted in the previous chapter is crucial as we try to attune to others, try to track their flight of song.

This is how attuning to ourselves directly impacts our ability to attune to others, a reciprocal attunement. Here's a trick (one of those "back pocket" tricks I use in nearly every single session), when I can attune to myself, it helps me attune to others, too. When a client shares that they feel stuck, overwhelmed, anxious, or depressed, I can sink into what that feels like for me, and I can use that to connect to what it might also feel like for them. When we can observe ourselves and reflect on ourselves, we can develop attunement for others. We can observe, "Oh, he's bouncing his leg up and down...when I bounce my leg up and down, it usually means I'm nervous or anxious," and we can translate that into, "You seem anxious as we talk about this." Or when I observe, "She looks insistent the way she's violently nodding her head as her husband talks...when I do that with my husband, it usually means I have a strong opinion about something, and he hasn't listened to my thoughts about it," and I can translate that into, "You seem like you have some strong thoughts about that—are those something you'd like to share?" My invitation to you here is to work to bring your full self into the counseling room, because in doing so, it helps us in so many ways. In this case specifically, it helps us attune to others.

I was meeting with a couple that I had worked with weekly for a few months; I knew them fairly well. They came into the session ready to dive into where we had left off the previous week, talking about the cycle of disconnection they can fall into during their busy work weeks. After about five minutes, something just felt "off." They were doing great work, going through the motions, having the conversation that seemed productive, but they seemed...different. I couldn't quite put my finger on what it was. I felt stumped.

One option was to do nothing, in fear that I had no clue what might be going on and trust that the path we were on was good enough. And it really was. It was good enough. Another option was to say something. To trust my attunement to the "something" and the "off" and simply say, "Something feels different or off today, is something going on?" When I was a new counselor, I would most definitely have gone the route of the first option. The feeling of something being "off" would have left as quickly as it came, like a cool breeze passing over our bodies. There it would have come, and there it would have gone. And that's okay. As beginners, we can only prioritize so many things at one time. The more confident I grew in bringing my authentic self into the counseling room, the more I recognized the flight of song as it drifted into the counseling room and grabbed hold of it. And you will, too. When it flits in, notice it. Trust it. Follow it. As you do, you will notice the depth you invite into the room.

When I took the second option of trusting that the "off" and "different" might mean something, I brought it into the room. And, in doing so, the clients ever so slowly and subtly looked at one another. I immediately thought, "Uh-oh...what kind of elephant did I invite into the room here?" The wife grabbed a tissue and looked at her husband. I looked at the "look." I took it in, and it communicated love, not disagreement. "Whew," I thought.

He started talking slowly and said, "Her dad had a massive heart attack last night, and she's not able to take off work. Her boss is gone, and she's in charge. She can't get on an airplane and go see him." His eyes also filled with tears. He reached for her hand, and they looked at one another. My heart sank deep, and I could feel my eyes filling with tears as well. We didn't need to continue our discussion about their disconnection; we needed to move into a different space. The space that felt "different" and "off" was true, and we went there. She shared how helpless she felt being so far away and wanting so desperately to be by her father's side. She shared she felt paralyzed by the fear she might lose him.

And if I'm being honest, I sat there quietly as they cried together, doing the work we had worked so hard to find over the last several weeks, and thought to myself, "Shit. I wonder how much I'd have missed if that breeze had floated right past. I wonder how many times I miss this." And the reality is, we likely miss quite a bit. But the encouragement here is to follow the flight of song, to trust the breeze as it passes, and to grab hold of the thought before it flits away—as much as you can and as often as you can. Listen to what people aren't saying, perhaps even more than you listen to the words they speak.

The true art of listening is hearing what is spoken underneath what clients are saying. There's an activity I do in an advanced clinical class to demonstrate attunement and the importance of noticing. In all honesty, it may be one of the most difficult tasks I ask of students. And frankly, it usually doesn't go well, in the best of ways. It involves more role-plays. I have the client or clients sit at the front of the room, ready to engage in some kind of heated argument about one thing or another (*the content doesn't matter*). Then I hand out earplugs. Yes, that's right—the counselors all get earplugs. They look at each other with both confusion and trepidation. Their task? Conduct a five-minute role-play wearing earplugs. When I say this, I hear the nervous and disbelieving laughter spread throughout the room. And I ask the clients to begin. What I see initially is sheer panic.

"What on earth do I say if I can't hear them say anything?"
"This is impossible."
"How do I do this without their words?"
"How do I even start?"

I see them literally lean in to try to hear the words, trying to beat the effort of the earplugs, trying to make out what the client is saying, to hear one word, any word, to grab ahold of. Desperate to hear the actual song. Here's the reality: many counselors, especially those just getting their feet wet, rely solely and desperately on the words clients say to inform them what to say next. So desperately. We hang on tightly to the content of what they speak to guide us to what we say next, like a neat little flow chart. They say this and then I say this and we follow that through the color-coded flow chart until the end of the session. The end. But when the words are gone, the students struggle. They try to read the lips, desperately searching in all the ways to find, hear, and see the words. The song itself. But the ask is to not hear the song but to follow the flight of it. Attunement is in the flight of the song.

> The true art of listening is hearing what is spoken underneath what clients are saying.

In a hushed voice, I share with the students, "Listen. In all the ways, with all the senses, earthly and spiritually, listen." When the words are no longer accessible, students struggle. A lot. Some of them straight up quit the activity. And that's okay! Some of them struggle and try so hard, and after they concede that this is really what is being requested of them, they begin to attune to body language, pauses in attacks, nuances in the room and between the clients. They shift gears completely. They begin to notice the shoulder shrugs, communicating confusion, frustration, giving up, or apathy. They start to see the head hanging low, communicating sadness, defeat, loneliness, or exhaustion. And they begin observing the clenched fist, communicating fear, anger, or desperation.

Students begin to notice annoyance or frustration and simply say, "That feels so frustrating for you." They see the client nod in agreement. Then the counselor attunes to self and identifies, "*When I feel frustrated, I can feel isolated,*" and then offers, "And that can feel isolating for you." And softening begins to happen! The client feels heard, but it wasn't their voice that was heard—it was their being. Their flight of song, not the song itself. Their being was seen, heard, and validated. And in doing that over and over again, clients feel attuned to. All across the room of role-plays, clients start talking softer, tears come, sessions slow down, and clients feel validated. *Without ever hearing a single word from the clients.*

Not every student loves this activity or feels successful at it. And the reality is that attuning to ourselves and to others takes practice and experience. It's a different kind of muscle, and it requires a different kind of permission. Following the flight of song might be the last thing anyone expects to tap into when signing up for a master's program in counseling. Education is historically so brain-focused: sharpen your mind, memorize data and techniques. I don't think I have ever received encouragement in anything intuition or attunement-related in education prior to graduate school. My guess is it's the same for you. My guess is that everyone entering a counseling program has already been conditioned to live only in their head. In class, in assignments, in supervision, and even in peer and professor conversations.

Moving From The Song To The Flight

My undergraduate degree is in natural science, and you better believe we didn't talk about attunement. I was taught facts, examination, scientific design, and experimentation. And if we involved humans, they were subjects from which we collected data. I learned to trust my brain, the facts, and the data, but I never even considered the integration of my thoughts, emotions, and gut feelings (perhaps this helps explain my abysmal under-grad GPA).

I was taught to define the black and white, only ask questions that can be answered with data and numbers, and if it can't be, ask a question or a hypothesis that can. And attunement, while based on taking in the information around us, isn't tangible, measurable, or easy to observe or learn. I never even considered that the beauty of the work of a counselor is something inside me already. I thought that I would learn all the skills that I needed to be a successful counselor from a book. I never considered that some of the things that matter the most can't be taught in a textbook.

Dear reader, not only does it matter, but it is incredibly meaningful to this work. That feeling you have about a client's anxiety matters. And I can't teach you that. That feeling you get when a client shares about their grief and you think it's likely connected to their grief from ten years ago—it matters, too. And I can't teach you that either. That wondering about the health of the parents' marriage when they bring in their twelve-year-old who is struggling in school—it matters, too. And I can't teach you that. It matters so much, it needs you to give it voice. Attunement is giving voice to what we notice in the room with clients. And what I can do is encourage you to follow it.

Giving voice to our attunement requires us to give ourselves permission to do so. I see this struggle with students all the time, hundreds of students, year after year. Enough people to say, hey reader, this is likely your struggle, too.

I was watching a brilliant and amazing clinician, Dana, in a counseling role-play. She was counseling a woman who presented as put together, wise, successful, accomplished, and a superwoman mother. Dana found herself confused about how she could help her. The client shared she wanted help with creating a schedule so she could make time for other things important to her. The counselor became increasingly disengaged from the woman, trying to keep up with her list of wants for the session. I watched the version of Dana that I know and love start to slowly leave the space. I slowed her down by interrupting and asking her, "Dana, what are you feeling? What is happening in the room right now?" And I paused. And waited. I saw her face go blank (or more blank than it already was). I saw tears form in her eyes, and her nervous fear spread pink across her neck and chest. I saw doubt and fear in the form of ghosts pass through her. They said, "You've said something stupid," or "How did you screw up this time?" and "You idiot, you missed something important." I can see these ghosts come.

I asked again, "Dana, listen to your gut. What is it saying?" The tears that were being held at bay started falling. She took a deep breath, and I could almost tangibly see her inviting her angels into the space and settling alongside me, almost as if whispering in encouragement, "Yeah, Dana, *what is your gut saying?*" I could see Dana shuttle from her head (where panic and comparison and fear live) into her heart, her gut, her intuition. And Dana said, "I feel sadness from her. I think she feels exhausted. With not only the tasks but the weight of everyone depending on her. She feels like Luisa in the movie Encanto.[4] She feels just like Luisa, carrying all the weight of others on her shoulders, and it's exhausting." I looked at Dana with joy-filled eyes in response to her astute and brilliant attunement and said, "Yessssssss....bring *that* into the room."

Counselors often need a little nudge to shuttle down into their own feelings and thoughts about clients. Far too often, we completely ignore our sense about things around us. When we give ourselves permission to listen to our wonderings, our ponderings, and our confusion, it is often right on target and can lead to really important spaces in the therapeutic relationship. Some of us are like Dana and, when given a little nudge, can attune to self and can attune to others.

Often, this attunement comes from years of reading others for our own safety and preservation. It comes from needing to learn this skill to make or keep others happy, to lessen the impact of our ghosts. Some of our clients are like this, too; they become so hypervigilant of the actions, motives, unspoken but felt expressions of others, and can sense things in others with ease, especially if nudged to do so. This is the group of people I fit into. And while some may view this as a superpower, like Luisa or Dana's client who reminds her of Luisa, it can be exhausting to be on alert at this level for so much of our lifetime.

> Counselors often need a little nudge to shuttle down into their own feelings and thoughts about clients and what they bring into the room. Far too often, we completely ignore our sense about things around us.

Others of us, when asked to shuttle down into our space of attunement, feel so lost and disconnected. This is the case with Josh. Josh was in a role-play with a couple, and they were covering quite a bit of ground with content. They were discussing a recent large purchase one partner had made without consulting the other. The wife was tearful when expressing that it felt like disrespect to her and she felt insignificant as a part of their partnership. As she spoke, she continued to cry. The counselor kept moving through the conversation, starting to initiate a dialogue about what dollar amount could be spent without any prior discussion.

I paused the counselor, inviting them to shuttle into their heart space, as I had done with Dana. "Josh, what are you feeling in the room right now? What do you see or sense is happening?" Josh gave me the blank stare that Dana did, but was confused about why I had stopped him. Josh responded with, "I'm not sure what you mean." I asked him, "Do you see that the wife is crying?" Josh looked towards the wife and, for the first time, saw her tears that had been there for quite some time. He wasn't about to reflect on what was happening in the room and felt disconnected from himself and the clients. He responded, saying he was confused and overwhelmed and didn't know what direction to take them next. He felt frozen and stuck, attunement far from reach.

If this feels like you, reader, it's okay. As we've moved through this book, we've come to understand there are a lot of really good reasons why some of us cannot attune to our own bodies. This, too, is the deep and important work of a counselor: getting in touch with your own thoughts and emotions. This isn't a place of failure; this is a place that needs nurturing and support. Because attunement, to yourself and to others, matters.

Attunement: What If I Get It Wrong?

Reader, I believe your attunement is part of the story of why

you're here. Why you are becoming a counselor, why you started or finished grad school, and why you picked up this book. I
believe you have a deep desire to learn and listen and have faith
in your desire to connect deeply with others. And some of you
have the road map, and some of you don't quite know how to
read the map yet. I'm here to tell you there are many ways to
get there, and there is no right way (which is true for so many
things in life and in counseling). One of the ways is to first get to
know *you* and attune to yourself. Part of that is done in our own
counseling, as counselors. Some of the best and most important
work is done in counseling.

As we all work to follow the flight of a song, sometimes
it's just plain hard. Or scary. Or both. I know when I started to
follow and trust this attunement, I felt it breeze in quickly, and
before it could settle, there was fear that I might get it wrong. Because of my particular brand of ghosts, I don't like being wrong.
Like, a lot. So I had many, many thoughts about what was happening in the room, but I zipped my lips tight when it came to
sharing them, fearing *that I might get it wrong*. Besides that, I was
told by a well-intentioned professor in grad school that it's wrong
for us to offer clients words about their experiences. That clients
know their experiences, and offering thoughts and ideas about
their experiences was putting words into their mouths.

But, the reality is, that's why they're in counseling. It hasn't
worked. They need help understanding and expressing their
thoughts and feelings in more meaningful and productive ways.
And attunement, when offered up, leads to deeper understanding, expression, and connection. So, let me encourage you:
please help the clients find the words that describe how they're

feeling. And risk getting it wrong. I get it wrong all the time; I really do. I'm not just saying that to make you feel like you're in good company. I really do get it wrong. And you know what? When I get it wrong, clients correct me and use their own words. They work with me to figure out what words fit for them a little bit better, and that can be even more meaningful when we co-create it together, with validation and connected exploration.

Attunement: What If I Get It Right?

The flip side of this is also true. Sometimes, I fear that in attuning to clients, *I might get it right.* I know that sounds silly, to be afraid that I might get it right, but it's true, and I bet you know what I'm talking about. Sometimes, when I listen to it and follow the flight of song, my attunement leads me to a sense of knowing that is deeply sad, or disconnected, or downright gut-wrenching.

I was working with a couple just the other day, and we were talking through a particular disagreement that they trip over quite a bit together. He travels a lot for work and is quite busy when he's away, leaving her with the kids and feeling disconnected from him. She took the children on a trip to another state and was busy and rarely connected with him. As they were processing this, underneath his anger and frustration that she did the same thing to him that he does to her, I sensed sadness, loneliness, and a feeling of being unloved.

Slowly and softly, I introduced this to him, that perhaps he was feeling pretty disconnected from her. Over the next few minutes, he began sharing, through tears, that he feels like this a lot in their marriage and often feels unlovable, disconnected, and not an equal partner in parenting. He handed over a bucket of deep longings that he'd been carrying for quite some time. And there was heaviness in what he shared.

For many new counselors (and sometimes for me, too!), these heavy emotions feel like quite the burden to sift through. If we don't feel ready or equipped to sift through them, many of us feel the attunement to this bucket of longings but run the other way, in fear we might be right and then have to sit in that muck with others. Sometimes, when we get it right, we can see and reveal a lot of stored-up pain.

Whether we get it wrong or get it right, attunement is a process that we have to practice, test, fail, confirm, or deny. And however it goes is okay. Whether we get it right or wrong, I encourage you to follow the flight of song. To let go of the need to follow the words of the song and be brave enough to notice and listen with the ear of your heart. In doing this and learning how to do this, I invite you to be kind to yourself. To go slow. And to try softer.

I see you, new counselor. I see you trying so hard to do all the things all at the same time to master and accomplish and be successful. Author Aundi Kolber[5] gives readers the permission to "try softer," and I'd like to extend this here to you, too. In seeking attunement to self and others, compassionately invite yourself to not try harder to learn all the words to all the songs required to become the counselor that you want to be, but to try softer. To adopt a more gentle approach with yourself as you learn. To slow down. To breathe. And to follow the flight of song.

CHAPTER ELEVEN

The Road Not Taken

I was sitting in the coffee shop the other day, sipping on a chai latte and reading—or, rather, trying to read. I was armed with my laptop and a good, inspiring book, hoping for a spark of creativity. As I sat there, I was easily distracted by everything around me, as per usual (is this all counselors?). There was a group of teenage girls that ordered some drinks with a billowed lid that seemed to be more whipped topping than anything else. There was a group of moms that seemed to have walked there, pushing their strollers with little ones. And there were the men with their laptops meeting with one person or another in a business meeting of some kind, or perhaps just pretending to be.

As I sat there, I noticed all the things. I was attuned to the movements, the feelings, the engagement tactics—and the avoidance tactics, too. I'm like a professional easily-distracted-noticer-of-all-the-things, even when I don't want to be. I also wondered about all the things. If attunement is in the noticing, curiosity is in the wondering about what we notice. Perhaps curiosity is what we do with attunement. As I sat there in the middle of the coffee shop, I couldn't help but both notice and wonder. A lot. While I didn't realize it at the time, clearly no productive work was going to be done. But then again, here I am writing about it. Inspiration is often found in the most curious places.

> If attunement is in the noticing, curiosity is in the wondering about what we notice. Perhaps curiosity is what we do with attunement.

I silently became part of each conversation happening around me. I sat there, taking it all in, letting myself get consumed by the conversations, the body language, the flight of song—the flight of so many songs all at once swirling around me. And do you know what I noticed? I noticed people who had arrived together paying very little attention to one another. I noticed people sharing a story (some of them quite intense) and then another person sharing *their* story and how similar or different it was from the original story. And back and forth, having a "conversation" but rarely listening or engaging in the depths of what the person was sharing.

As I sat there, I noticed the group of moms. One was sharing seemingly brand new information about her in-laws unexpectedly moving into town soon. Another woman rolled her eyes, another said something about boundaries, and another was too distracted by her crying baby to hear. I heard the first woman say, "I'm actually excited for a built-in babysitter," and they all laughed and shared a murmur that communicated, "It's not like that." I noticed the woman pull into herself; her whole demeanor changed in the blink of an eye, and she quickly changed the subject. My first reaction was deep irritation. I wanted to butt in on my clearly-I'm-better-than-you soapbox and say, "Hey, do you not see your friend here? Did you see her become less of herself when you didn't really hear her? How about you stop jumping to conclusions and just *listen*?"

Then, the other layer settled in for me, too. As I watched

her excitement disappear, I felt her sadness. I felt her disappointment. I wanted to kneel on the floor in front of her, set my hands on her tired legs, and whisper to her:

"It's okay if life feels hard right now."
"Do you have anyone you can really talk to?"
"What weighs the most heavily on you right now?"
"What excites you about them moving closer?"
"Tell me more."

My heart was on fire for the underlying emotions that are easily missed if we aren't curious with one another, if we aren't slicing emotions thinner and being curious about them. Sometimes we can just be so focused on a certain direction, a certain goal, or a particular topic of conversation that we miss the opportunities that are presented in the space of right here and right now.

> Too many of us seek to listen to people solely with the intent to respond rather than to understand and be curious.

In those coffee shop conversations, I was curious about what the mom was hearing about her in-laws. I was curious about how her experience and relationships could be so different from someone else's. I was wondering about the desire for a babysitter and how often she gets time away from her children. I pondered about her identity apart from being a mom. I found myself distracted by how much all of these coffee shop conversations aren't really conversations at all, but people sharing one thing, followed by another share, followed by another share. It made me wonder how little people pay attention to one another.

Too many of us seek to listen to people solely with the intent to respond rather than to understand and be curious. And gosh, it made me wonder how often that happens in the counseling room as well.

The Path Most Traveled

The truth is, I'm guilty of this, too. While I am a noticer and get curious sometimes, I'm also guilty of running straight over people and not being curious at all about what they're sharing. In the spirit of getting through to the plan or the goal or what we came here to talk about, I can be so self-absorbed or goal-accomplishing, and already writing the session notes in my head. Curiosity is something I have to be aware of and strive for, and it continues to be a growth edge for me. Maybe it is for you, too.

Curiosity is often the path less traveled. Most often, we jump right on that well-worn pathway of assumptions about our clients and their experiences rather than taking the other path, the one that leads to wondering and pondering and curiosity. But the reality is, this is quite the dilemma for us counselors.

We want to be experts, have niches, know things, develop empathy and tools, and have direction. And the truth of the matter is that those things are important. It's exciting, rewarding, and validating to be with a client and have the experience of feeling, "Oh! I've had a client kind of like this before, and I can do/ask/use what worked before." And it often does! The more I learn about a particular theory that I use with couples, the more I see the predictable patterns show up in their interactions. I can easily identify the "pursuer" and the "withdrawer"[1] and can therefore outline a cycle of disconnection and know the pathway to connection. And it feels good! And clients love it. Right up until I get lost because it's not *quite* like the last client. Or what appeared to be a "withdrawer" was just someone exhausted in their role of pursuing. And my unconscious desire to hurry ahead and jump to the next step runs straight into a wall. Been there, done that. Still do that. I can get so caught up in doing what's next or nodding my head because I know what clients mean or are going to say next, and I pat myself on the back for being "attuned to them."

But attunement is only half of the story here. The other half is curiosity. Curiosity is in wondering about what we've attuned to. It's seeing a fork in the road and not just rushing down the one we know because we know it and it's familiar and it feels good. Nope. Not that pathway. It's actually in taking the other road. The one that isn't filled with "yes" head nods but with head tilts that communicate, "Huh, I wonder..."

The Path Less Traveled

There's a poem by Robert Frost called "The Road Not Taken"[2] that talks about traveling down the road of "I wonder" that is less traveled than the "I know this" road. As you read it, think about how often, as a counselor, you jump to something other than curiosity: to answers, justifications, solutions, and responses. As I read it now, as I place it in this spot, I'm reminded of a recent visit with my husband's 90-year-old grandmother in the hospital. She was sharing that she's outliving all of her friends, even some of her children, and how sad and depressing it feels to be left alone, and that sometimes she wishes "God would just take her." Out of my mouth came phrases like, "You're surrounded by grandkids" and "You're not alone at all" and "You've lived such a meaningful life," providing her with reassurance, reminders, and justifications. I didn't listen to her truth, to her fears, to her loneliness.

Reader, I've been a counselor for nearly half my lifetime, and I still missed the opportunity to connect, to listen with the ear of my heart, and to be present. I missed it. The song came, and not only did I not follow the flight of it, but I asked her to sing a completely different song. And I started to sing it for her. I took the well-worn path rather than being curious about her words, about her heart. As I drop this smack dab right here in this chapter, I've invited myself to be curious about how differently that conversation might have gone had I wondered out loud with her and let her lead me down the road not taken.

"The Road Not Taken"
By Robert Frost

Two roads diverged in a yellow wood,
And sorry I could not travel both
And be one traveler, long I stood
And looked down one as far as I could
To where it bent in the undergrowth;

Then took the other, as just as fair,
And having perhaps the better claim,
Because it was grassy and wanted wear;
Though as for that the passing there
Had worn them really about the same,

And both that morning equally lay
In leaves no step had trodden black.
Oh, I kept the first for another day!

Yet knowing how way leads on to way,
I doubted if I should ever come back.

I shall be telling this with a sigh
Somewhere ages and ages hence:
Two roads diverged in a wood, and I—
I took the one less traveled by,
And that has made all the difference.

The work of a counselor requires us to not take the well-worn pathway of the coffee shop conversations, but to take the road less traveled, the one that involves questions and wonderings and head tilts in wonder much more than head nods in confirmation. Listen more and talk less. Give space for the other to share and struggle and show up however they want and need to show up. The concept of listening to understand, in counseling and in life outside of counseling, too often gets the credit for being an important part of the healing process. The reality is that the understanding part is not the endpoint at all. The understanding part is a false endpoint to connection. True connection is in the wondering: the desire to know more, connect deeper, and be curious about the depths of fears, joys, and longings.

Be Curious Together

If you are anything like me, the coffee shop conversations that can fill life are not at all life-giving for us. We, collectively, long for deeper, more intimate, meaningful conversations. I know I do; I bet you do, too. And so do our clients. We yearn to be pursued and asked about our longings, dreams, hopes, and fears. And I know you landed here because you want to do this for clients.

When I talk to you before or after you've entered graduate school, you tell me you want to be here, in this field, in graduate school, to help people. If I dig deeper and slice the "help people" thinner and let you wonder about this answer for yourself, you often say, "I want to be a counselor because I'm curious about people" and "I'm in this field so I can observe and wonder about people." Because underneath the expression of "I want to help people" are flights of song that include deep wondering and deep curiosity about people. You long to know about their brokenness, their pain, their resiliency, their grief, and their fight for deeper connections. Many of us counselors find great joy in being curious. The reason we show up every day, every hour. And I love that about you, counselor. I love when you slow down and give yourself permission to be wildly curious. Being a counselor is about giving yourself permission to wonder about all the things and be deeply curious about the inner workings and wonderings of a client's heart.

> The concept of listening to understand too often gets the credit for being an important part of the healing process. The reality is that the understanding part is not the endpoint at all. The understanding part is a false endpoint to connection. True connection is in the wondering: the desire to know more, connect deeper, and be curious about the depths of fears, joys, and longings.

Part of the work of a counselor is being *curious together* with your clients. There's an activity I do in classes that helps demonstrate the power of sharing the reciprocal nature of counseling, health, and healing. It simply involves passing a ball back and forth while doing a counseling role-play. Clients love to pass the metaphorical ball to us, to give us control, responsibility, and power. It's our job to catch the ball, wonder about it as we collectively look at it, and then give it back. When we keep it, tuck it away, and hold it tightly in our hands, we can feel burdened by this weight. Reader, please don't keep the ball. Pass it back and forth. Together. When we can be curious together in the counseling space with our clients, we get to co-create. We invite them to call forth their creativity and gifts and wonderings. And the cultivation of curiosity calls for the creative wonderings of both the client and you in a reciprocal nature. A co-creation of healing. And isn't that the most beautiful work of counseling in the first place? Being curious is an act of inviting the client to be really present with you in the process. Inviting them to share more, to explore more, and to *be curious together.*

It Has Made All The Difference

I was talking to a new therapist, and she was racing through her case conceptualization, treatment plan, and planned interventions and getting ready to share her stuck places with me in supervision when I asked her, "What makes you curious about this client?" She stopped. And laughed. She literally laughed. Not a nervous chuckle. She belly laughed. Then she said, "Michelle, I don't even know. I haven't even thought about it." The question took her so much by surprise. So, in my most-Michelle way, I sat quietly and invited her to answer the question about her client, who had lost her husband to cancer in the months before.

She became quiet and then shared, "I wonder what motivates her to get up in the morning. I wonder who she texts throughout the day. I wonder what her evenings look like alone.

I wonder how much she misses her husband. I wonder what it feels like to cook for one instead of two." And this amazing counselor rested in her curiosities for a long time, and she said, "The fog just lifted." For her, being curious brought such a sense of clarity. She didn't need to know what was next. She didn't need to know all the answers she thought she should know. She could simply *not* have all the answers or know the next step or twelve steps, and she could just rest in curiosity.

When we can spend our sessions resting in curiosity, we can look forward to what is next with anticipation and curiosity. And when we remain curious, it keeps us excited about this work for the long haul. It comes from curiosity. It frees us to thrive instead of simply survive. And when we thrive, we do better work. We help people. And helping people is what called you here in the first place.

Curiosity serves as a path less traveled for us counselors. Curiosity keeps us focused on the discovery of the uniqueness of our clients. It's okay to not know all the time. Instead of feeling like you have to nod "yes" to show that you understand and have earned some "I've arrived" badge as a counselor, it's okay to say, "What do you mean by *good*? What does it mean that things are *better*?" To keep following the path of curiosity. Curiosity doesn't ask a lot of us; it just asks us to see where the next clue leads us and follow the trail like a scavenger hunt to see what is next, just one little hint at a time.

Every day, as travelers, we are invited into the yellow wood and presented with diverging roads. The work of a counselor requires us to make constant decisions about which path to take. Many clients come into our offices because the path they themselves have taken over and over again hasn't resulted in the change they hoped for or desired. So they feel stuck, lost, and alone. We, as counselors, take their metaphorical hand and guide them down diverging paths at every turn.

The paths we take won't all be the best ones, and that's okay. They won't all lead to magic healing and profound realization, and that's okay, too. They won't all lead to breaths of hope, healing tears, or client affirmations. But sometimes they do. And sometimes, when we can show up as our authentic self, trusting our intuitions and moving towards connection, we can lead them down the road less traveled. Take that road. Have the courage to be curious. Take the unknown path that wants the wear, that yearns to be explored, to find the undisturbed beauty that awaits. Take the one that is less obvious. Go there. Reader, I believe in you. I believe your curiosity is leading you to uncharted roads and that those roads will make all the difference.

CHAPTER TWELVE

Listen Within

There's an old, tried-and-true activity I do with nearly all of my students in class each year. Those who have had me in class before groan under their breath when I introduce it. They know where it leads. But, for the sake of the activity and the learning opportunity, humor me here for a second. On a piece of paper, or in the margins here, or even in your head, list the three most important relationships in your life. Don't think too hard; I'm not asking you to prioritize your four children or anything like that. Just make a quick list of those most important to you. Right now. Do it. Just pause from reading for one moment, close your eyes, and think about who those people are.

Okay. Did you do it? Do it!

Here's the kicker question: are you on your list? This is the point where all the students groan collectively and share things like, "Well, I didn't know I could put myself on the list," or "That was a trick question." And there are always a few people who are on to me and did put themselves on the metaphorical list but then struggle to share how that actually shows up in their day-to-day lives. Others have an idea of what it looks like and feels like to prioritize our needs, especially as a helper. Some of those refer to things like journaling, getting a massage, or running... you know, the go-to self-care responses (insert eye roll here).

The Road To Burnout

It's tricky being a counselor. We pour into others all day long. We pour out love and compassion and authenticity and vulnerability. We provide unconditional positive regard. We provide a safe space. We validate and empathize hundreds of times a day in a multitude of different ways because we've learned that everyone is different and has different needs. And so we adjust, we cater, we move as clients need, and we learn to figure them out just a little bit more each session. This work brings us great joy. And this work is completely and utterly exhausting. Sometimes deeply, soul-level exhausting. I don't say that to complain; that is just the way it is when we sit with so much pain and suffering. Our hearts hold it, our souls hold it, our bodies hold it. We feel honored to hold it. We feel honored to sit in these spaces. It is also quite fulfilling, which brings us back day after day—until one day, we feel like we may not have anything else to give...to ourselves or others. And we feel completely empty.

Just a few weeks ago, I received a text from a therapist I supervise who has been out of school for three years and is nearing licensure. The text said:

"Without freaking you out...I think I should tell you that I'm pretty sure I've reached burnout. I felt like I needed someone else to know. Full honesty: just telling you this feels like a failure. I realize that's not true, but it sure feels like it."

This person is just like you and me, reader. She is compassionate, busy, and aware of the need to take care of herself. She is a brilliant, deep healer and is really good at her work with clients. And, she found herself empty. She knew she needed to invite someone into the space with her, but doing so made her feel like a failure. The very act of reaching out and telling a safe person, "I'm tired and exhausted and I don't know what to do," made her feel like a failure. Reading those words did make me freak out on the inside, but not for the reasons she thought they would. I felt the "freak out" deep in my gut as I thought to myself...me too. I felt like her words just about knocked me over because I know that feeling so deeply, and she was brave enough to put into words what I had not. I let my pride, ego, and drive to succeed prevent me from sharing those very words with others. I'll avoid my soapbox about how extremely sad it is that society has created such a mess of people that we're afraid to share our struggles with others.

As I sat with tears in my eyes, staring at the phone with her text, I validated her, sent her love and hugs, and asked her, "What do you need?" As I pushed the send button, I asked myself the same question. She shared that she needed sleep, some quiet time, a good, long walk, and to be free from her adult responsibilities for a while. She said she needed some "self-care." I needed that, too. But as I pondered that question, "What do you need?" I felt like what she said she needed wasn't enough. We needed something more than that, something deeper. We need self-care that is more like self-care than what we've come to know self-care to be.

> I already know what this self-care chapter says, and I already know I'm not living up to the standards that I should be in that regard, so no thank you, I'll pass on the large helping of shame.

It's become cliche in this line of work to mention the phrase "self-care." We know we need to take care of ourselves. We know if we don't, it will lead to burnout. We know it's important to carve out time, to lean in, to show up, and and and and... and yet it's hard. It's hard because we love people, and we love showing up for others. We get paid (or will soon) to do it, and we do it in our personal lives. We are the friend people call up and lean on (and we love it!). We host parties, we have play dates with our kids, we volunteer at church, we serve the community, we bring meals to others, we take care of our elderly neighbors. We love others, and we do it well. What we don't do as well is turn our attention to ourselves.

Part of me almost decided not to include a chapter on self-care in this book because of the cliche of it and the eye roll that ensues after hearing the overused phrase, especially in helping professions like counseling. I do the same thing. I already know what the whole chapter says in chapters about self-care; we've read it a thousand times before. People become numb to the idea of self-care, and many want to skip the chapter altogether. Literally. I don't want to read another chapter on self-care. I already know what this self-care chapter says, and I already know I'm not living up to the standards that I should be in that regard, so no, thank you, I'll pass on the large helping of shame.

Just in case you've been living under a rock or haven't gotten that far in your master's program yet, let me catch you up—it won't take long. You should take care of yourself. If you don't, you'll get burned out. And when you get burned out, you won't do very good work, and you won't feel good about the work you do. You know, "You can't fill up others from your own empty cup" sort of stuff. The basic articles/podcasts/blogs suggest you should do yoga, meditate, go for a run, and journal, and then you'll be a healthier, more well-balanced person. And some of those things work for some people some of the time.

The more advanced articles poo-poo those things and go a little bit deeper, suggesting that many of those are just stereotypical suggestions and what self-care really looks like is emotional boundaries, paying your bills, good sleep habits, nutrition, preventative healthcare, and professional development. And those things are good, too. I hope we all do those things. But with my mammogram scheduled for tomorrow and my colonoscopy scheduled in several weeks, I wouldn't for a hot second put them in the category of "self-care," even though that's exactly what it is: it is caring for myself, at least physically. But it's not the self-care I had in mind.

Heart Shift

True self-care isn't about something you can do or just check off your to-do list. It's not more sleep, some quiet time, and a good, long walk—although those things can be an important part of it. It's not something I can even answer for you. I wish I could. I wish I could do that for you and for me. But I can't say, "Just do _____ and that's the way to self-care." Although I know intimately what that's like to just want that answer. Please, tell me what to do to take care of myself, and I'll do that and then check it off and move on. That might work for about three hours or even three days before something sets me off, and I'm right back where I started. And usually, when I ask that question, I'm already in desperate need of self-care. My walks and meditations and massages only got me so far, and my body and mind and spirit desperately need something more. Something deeper.

Because true, deep self-care isn't an act; it isn't a quick fix or an item on a to-do list to get checked off. It's really super ambiguous. I'm sorry. I wish it were easy. I wish it were easy and clear and direct. I wish the ten-step guide to self-care was a one-hour lecture I could give to students in the classroom, and then everyone would just know how to take care of themselves, but it's not that easy. It's complicated and ambiguous and requires a lot of work. The best self-care is a way of being. It's a heart shift. It's making shifts in our values, our worth, ourselves, and our relationships with others. It's at the very heart of the work we do with our own clients. We have a deep desire for them to dig deep, to examine, and to listen with the ear of their hearts to their own heart. To your own heart, reader. Self-care is listening within—to you. It's answering the question that I asked of that clinician and myself, "What do you need?" Deeper than "I need rest." What will that rest give you? What kind of rest? What is it that you deeply need?

| The best self-care is a way of being. It's a heart shift.

In these surface-level definitions of self-care, there's something big missing. The "big missing" is you. We take this advice from others about us without checking in with ourselves to see if it's what we need. If our mind, body, heart, and soul actually need whatever we've been told we should do or probably need. Of course, our bodies need vegetables and movement and love, but I believe, at a visceral level, what we need the most is to ask ourselves what we need.

Author Taylor Elyse Morrison describes self-care as the process of listening within and responding in the most loving way possible.[1] Listening within. The listening part is the "big missing". The part of the process that many of us neglect because the world is really good at telling us what we need to care for ourselves. But in that process, we can forget to filter it through our season of life, our lived experiences, our financial capacity, and our abilities. I think a lot of people—well-meaning, smart people—forget to listen to themselves. I forget to listen sometimes. When I'm tired, I think I should probably go for a walk or tune into the latest Netflix craze. Or I should wake up early and work out without listening to my body and hearing if maybe it's too tired to wake up early and what it really needs is sleep. Or I can so easily just do the next thing on my to-do list or expectation list without pausing and asking myself what I need.

It's Up To You

A few weeks ago, I had a full, tough day. The type of day where some bigger and more unusual things were adding to the heaviness of my heart. I had a hard session with a couple (I gave myself a solid C-) that went longer than I expected, which made me late in bringing my daughter to an important, non-typical doctor's appointment. On the way to the appointment, I was trying to process the session while also helping her process her fear and anxiety about the appointment. While driving and dual-processing with her and me, I got a call informing me there was a significant medical emergency in our counseling office, and I needed to close the office and connect with each of our several clinicians to let them know. I was stressed and exhausted and not listening within at all. I'm not very good at listening within because, frankly, I'm afraid of what I might hear. I'm afraid my need will be too great, my failure will be too loud, and my insecurities will be too much. And then, if I hear it, I'll either need to do something about it or ignore it again, so I might as well just keep ignoring it. It's easier that way. So I stop listening within. I'm not even sure when it happened, but along the way, I became really good at listening beyond and really terrible at listening within.

But here's the reality: if I don't listen within and respond in the most loving way possible, nobody else will. And I think that's part of the trouble sometimes—we keep waiting for someone else to take care of us and meet our needs. I used to think my husband needed to do this, but he doesn't have a crystal ball that he can look into and discover my innermost needs. For a long time, I kept waiting. And sometimes he'd get it right, and sometimes he wouldn't. As therapists, we generally love to take care of others, and it's part of what draws us to this profession. But the person who bears the responsibility of our self-care is us. Sometimes I still wait around for someone to do it for me, with me, to me. Just take care of all my unspoken needs, please. Sometimes it feels like I'm still a small child who needs someone to care for my every need. And that's because many of us have ongoing open attachment wounds. I know I do. And I know some of you do, too. You tell me, through tears and perceived failures and imposter syndrome and countertransference, that many of us are waiting for a parent figure (partner, friends, children...often not a parent at all anymore) to soothe and care for us. Sometimes, that's actually what draws us to becoming a counselor.

> But here's the reality: if I don't listen within and respond in the most loving way possible, nobody else will.

We kept waiting for someone to take care of us, but they never came, so we want to make sure we are there for others to give that to them. But self-care is different; it's from within. It has to be. Self-care is part of the process we undertake of becoming our own caretakers, our own parents. To us. It's when we stop waiting for someone else to take care of our inner needs and our heart longings, and we learn that we need to do that for ourselves. For you. For me. I am in a constant state of learning that permission already exists for me to take care of myself. I am the parent. You are the parent. No more waiting for someone else to take care of you.

I think sometimes we keep waiting because we don't know that permission slip exists within ourselves, and we don't know that we are deserving of care and love—right now. Our lived experiences and our ghosts continue to follow us and remind us that we don't deserve to be cared for in the deep ways that we need. But you are worth it. You can provide for yourself in all the ways you most need to be taken care of, or begin working in that direction. No more waiting for someone else.

You can listen within and answer the question: what do you need?

You Can't Do It Alone

While we are learning to take care of ourselves, we also need help from others. It's quite the paradox, really. Both the need for others and the suggested independence. The dependence and the encouragement to do for ourselves. This is a paradox within self-care, too. As we learn to become our own selves and take care of and love our own selves, it's also helpful if we have others to help us learn how to do this. No wonder it's confusing and ambiguous—*because it is*.

A counselor called me in quite a panic because she received a client referral from our clinical manager, who suggested she would be a perfect fit. The clinician needs more clients and felt obligated to take this client. I simply asked the counselor, "Do you want this client?" I encouraged her to listen within. The phone went quiet. And she quietly said, "Not even a small part of me wants to take on this client." And I said, "Is that an option for you?" (knowing full well that it was an option), and with shock in her voice, she responded, "Really? I can do that?" Yes, counselor, you can listen within and respond to your own needs in the most loving way possible. *Please* listen within and respond in the most loving way possible. Maybe that means canceling all of your clients for a week when you're sick. Maybe that means saying "no" when the "shoulds" tell you to say yes. Maybe it's scheduling a four-day weekend every few months. Maybe it's making sure you have a one-hour lunch break every day.

This counselor, just like you and me, needed someone to consistently give her permission to listen, to honor, and to respond accordingly. We need that, too, as we learn to listen within, take care of ourselves, and parent ourselves well.

And it's okay if we need others to help us listen within. When I teach the practicum and internship courses, I start every single class with a shared self check-in.

How are you showing up today?
What are your supervision needs today?
What is one emotion to describe your day/week?

This helps students (and me) to listen within and respond in the most loving way possible. Sometimes, as I answer those questions alongside them, I realize I'm irritable or tired or energized or thoughtful. And knowing that matters. Just like in previous chapters, where learning to process your own thoughts and feelings can help you attune to others, connecting to your feelings here and listening within is a prerequisite for self-care. The deep, heart shift self-care that we really need that can sustain us. When we can listen within and sink into that heart shift, I can respond to myself (and others) in the most loving way possible. Once I know this, I can make changes in my day based on this information. If I listen within and discover that I'm irritable, I can make sure I do things a little differently throughout the day. I can bite my tongue, I can filter my words, I can ask for kindness and grace. I can prioritize my own needs. The attunement and listening within allow a response, a shift. And this response is a loving care of ourselves.

Listen And Answer

I was doing monthly supervision with a clinician a few years ago. I started the supervision time with a check-in, and she shared she was incredibly overwhelmed and felt really emotional and dysregulated. I asked her, "What do you need?" and waited. I watched as she closed her eyes and began to listen within. As she did, tears started rolling down her cheeks. As she gently wiped them away, she said, "I need to not be here today doing this, but since that's not an option, I'm not sure." I paused her and asked, "Is that an option for you? Can we not meet today?" Her eyes opened, and I simply asked for her permission to respond to herself in the most loving way possible. Through tears, she shared, "I'd love to meditate and do yoga right now and listen more." I simply said, "Okay." We rescheduled. She shut off the lights in her counseling office, laid on the floor, let herself cry and process, and gave herself exactly what she needed.

> She goes within but doesn't go within to *listen*; she goes within to escape and withdraw from others. This is not the same thing. Going within invites you into a beautiful conversation, a heart posture that allows you to truly listen to what your heart needs underneath the phony layers of fake self-care.

I think many times, we listen within, and then we stop there. We hear ourselves, know our needs, and then brush them off because we need to be strong, or we need to show up, or we need to show up a certain way, or we feel like a failure if we don't do/finish/power through. But both parts of the phase are incredibly important. If we listen within and hear but do not respond in the most loving way possible, self-care is not present. It's almost as if we participate in self-neglect if we listen and don't respond. A lack of listening within, paired with self-neglect, is a perfect recipe for burnout. It is crucial to both listen within and respond in the most loving way possible.

The Deeper Needs

Dear reader, let me be super clear about this for a minute. My daughter would call this my "serious voice," the one where I'm trying to make a point so my voice changes, slows, and has a strong desire for poignancy. You don't have to be exhausted to be worthy of rest. Self-care isn't something that needs to be earned. You are worth whatever work you might still need to do to become a healthy counselor. To listen within. You are worth listening to, and you are definitely worth responding to in the most loving and tender way possible.

> You don't have to be exhausted to be worthy of rest.
> Self-care isn't something that needs to be earned.

When I talked further with the clinician who texted me and vulnerably shared that she was burned out, we discovered something deeper. After slicing her need for rest thinner and thinner, when she deeply listened within, she learned that her needs were not what she thought they were. When she shared that she needed "sleep, some quiet time, a good, long walk, and to be free from her adult responsibilities for a while," it was masking her deeper needs. I invited her to dig deeper, to listen within, into what those needs meant.

> What will _____ (sleep, quiet time, long walk) provide for you?
> What kind of _____ (sleep, quiet time, etc.) is it that you need?
> What is it that you deeply need from _____ (sleep, rest, etc.)?
> What caused you to need _____ (rest, quiet, solitude)?

And the answers to those questions revealed a deeper need: the heart longings that had gone unmet. While this clinician may have also needed sleep and quiet time, what she really, truly needed was for people to see her suffering, to see her drowning. What she needed was help—the opposite of quiet time in some ways. This clinician's ghosts often tell her to retreat and hide when she feels overwhelmed, and she often listens. She goes within but doesn't go within to *listen*; she goes within to escape and withdraw from others. This is not the same thing. Going within invites you into a beautiful conversation, a heart posture that allows you to truly listen to what your heart needs underneath the phony layers of fake self-care.

Do *you* know what *you* need? When you listen within, is there a list of unspoken longings that need tending to? My hunch is the answer for each one of us is yes. I wonder if those questions might serve as a guide for you, too, as you search for the deeper needs that have gone unmet. On my drive home each day from work, I strive to search my soul for these needs. A self-directive "Listen within, Michelle, what is it that I deeply, truly need right now". I've discovered it is a crucial practice to help me be more present for myself and those I love. When you listen within, what are those needs? Circle back to the list of questions and wonder about these needs for you.

I want to deeply encourage you to bring in tenderness and compassion as you become. As you find or remind yourself of your worth. As you listen within, may you be ever so loving and tender with yourself. It's a practice, this deep form of self-care. It's not the list you can read in an article or in a book chapter. There's no quick fix. I'm sorry. Maybe that's why we want to skim over these chapters and articles, because we know deep down that the surface-level changes don't work. We skip them because we know this work requires deep change and, if you're anything like me, sometimes we want to flat-out avoid this part of the learning process.

This process of becoming a healthy counselor requires that you believe you are worth self-care. That you believe you deserve it and then act on it because you know your worth and you believe you are worth the effort to listen and respond with great love and care. It requires deep work, sometimes (oftentimes?)

counseling through our own traumas and ghosts so we can quiet the noise and listen within. I invite you, reader, as I lay down my serious voice and opt for my loving and tender voice, to take care of yourself. You are worth it. And as you learn how to do this well, as the seasons of being a counselor ebb and flow, that you come back to you. That the "big missing" is no longer you because you've spent time practicing listening within and, ultimately, with love and compassion, respond in the most loving way possible. To you. For you.

PART THREE

Belonging

"True belonging doesn't require you to change who you are; it requires you to be who you are."

Brené Brown[1]

CHAPTER THIRTEEN

Fight Song

I t was a telehealth session over the computer. I pushed the "end meeting" button, shut my laptop, and, to the silent room, whispered, "fuck!"

I remember the sun was shining bright through the nearby window, and it felt like such a contrast to what I was feeling in the room. The room was decorated to be inviting, warm, and cozy. I felt darkness. Regret. Stupidity. I wasn't sure whether to be angry and string a line of curse words together or to sit and cry. The session was terrible. It was the worst session in the history of sessions. In prior sessions, the wife had (quite willingly and with apparent ease) shared with me that she wasn't enjoying our sessions. The husband tried to soften her words, but he was too late. She thought I was stupid. She thought this was worthless. Therapy was a waste of money. Did I have a real degree? Do I even have training to do this work? Okay, she didn't say those *exact* words, but those are the messages my heart heard.

In reality, she probably said something more like, "This isn't as effective as we hoped," or "We're going to take a break from counseling for a while," or "I don't think we are the best fit for each other," or "I don't think you understand me." I'm not exactly sure what she said because my brain immediately knew where it was going. I was getting fired by a client. Once I knew that part, the ghosts wrote the rest of the script that I heard. And it was excruciating. I had to sit there and listen and be professional. They were firing me anyway, so couldn't I just pretend like we had a bad connection and push the "end meeting" button now?

Anger could have easily taken over because I had worked my butt off for them. I had poured so much of my time and energy into them! I had worked so hard to connect with the wife, to validate her fears, to normalize her concerns, and to make sure she felt seen. I had worked so hard to soften her so her husband could see her deeply buried longings and hurts. With great effort, I had worked to get the husband to come out of his cave where he felt safe and protected. I had poured so much into helping him have the courage to share his fears. I had worked so hard.

Maybe I had worked too hard? Or maybe I hadn't done enough. Maybe when she left that session crying and we had run out of time, I should have done something more. Maybe when he finally shared his pain, I should have held them differently? Or stopped him? Or encouraged him to share more? Maybe I didn't do enough? Either way, the tears came, and I was convinced I had either done too much or hadn't done enough. And that quickly and easily translated in my heart to both "I'm too much" and "I'm not enough" at the same time. I'm not sure how that's even possible, but I held both of those realities together.

This story here represents my feelings many times. This isn't my one and only "worst session in the history of the world." I have had what feels like a million. I have these sessions. I fight these battles. I fight against comparison. And imposter syndrome. And ghosts. And distractions. And it's exhausting. I think if I have a full week of clients, I'm bound to have one (at least) absolutely horrible session. And I know just because it feels horrible doesn't mean it was horrible. But then again, sometimes it does.

I know many of you feel like you're too much; you feel like maybe you've worked too hard or said too much or pushed too much. I also know many of you feel like you're not enough. You didn't do enough, didn't say enough, didn't show up enough. I know, deeply, I do. I know a few of the battles that some of you fight every day. I know the ghosts and the imposter syndrome create a list of words and phrases that you have on repeat that run like a script through your head and seep down to your heart as well. And you believe those phrases to your core. And I also know it's not limited to "I'm not enough" and "I'm too much." Some of your phrases include, "I'm a fraud," and "I don't know anything," and "I'm too broken," and "I'm too scared." The phrases are specific to you, your ghosts, your imposter syndrome, and your deeply hidden fears.

Don't Believe Your Lies

And that's the nature of counseling. This work is both relentlessly and unexpectedly amazing and tests our enoughness and our fears at every corner. It tests our self-talk statements and confirms those statements far too often. I've had to work very diligently over my lifetime and my career to invite the angels into those spaces. The ghosts sure can fill the room in the blink of an eye. I have to intentionally make space for the angels, too. Our angels help us feel rooted, grounded, loved, appreciated, and seen.

The angels help us rewrite the scripts we play in our head that tell us all kinds of things about who we are, what our worth is, and whether or not we can do this work. They help us see we are not too much and are exactly enough. These angels who show up say, "You are good as you are," and "I can do this," and "I'm not responsible for making people happy." These angels remind you, "You can do this," and "Hard doesn't mean you can't do it," and "It's okay to cry," and "It's okay to struggle; it doesn't mean you won't figure it out—it means you're human."

> This field requires us to be our own cheerleader sometimes.

The more I live this life as a human among other humans doing the best we can day after day, the more I've come to realize we all need to hear and be reminded to battle our negative self-talk statements. We all need more angels to battle the ghosts. I think this is human nature—not just for counselors. But here in this book, this is just for you. For you who are just beginning or trying to find your way, while also trying to figure out what it means to be a counselor. This book, this chapter, is just for you, like a little love letter from me to you. And my deep hope for you, reader, is that this chapter and this book serve as a layer (or fifteen) of reminders of your worth, value, success, depth, creativity, safety, humor, and kindness. This field requires us to be our own cheerleader sometimes. We sit alone with clients hour after hour without them reminding us how amazing we are, how much we're changing their lives, how meaningful it is to sit in the muck with them. Sometimes they share that with us, and it feels good and validating, but other times, we have to do that for ourselves. We have to remember that we can do this. We are

_____ just the way we are, day after day. Sure, learning and growing are important and part of our ongoing process. But at our core, deep there in the middle where nobody sees, that part there is enough.

Our Self-Talk Becomes True

In my early twenties, I attended a series of leadership trainings. During one of these trainings, we were asked to participate in an activity. Someone would stand and hold out their arm parallel to the ground, and the goal was to hold it solidly while someone else pushed it down toward the ground. The activity consisted of two parts: during the first part, the person holding out their arm would say out loud positive self-talk statements: "I can resist! I am holding strong! I am powerful! I will do this!" while resisting the opposing force of the push. What we saw was people solidly holding their arms out straight, resisting the force of the other, and acting out what they were saying. Okay, that makes sense.

In the second part of the activity, the person held out their arms, and the other person resisted, but this time, the person would say negative self-talk statements. "I can't do this. I won't resist. I am weak. I'm not good at this." I sat there, amazed at how much people couldn't resist the push. Their arms began dropping towards the ground as they tried to fight against it but continued to say negative self-talk statements. Our bodies literally listen to the words coming out of our mouths. We are literally influenced by the words we say about ourselves, to ourselves.

I was a skeptic, convinced their arms had become tired from the efforts of the first round, so they couldn't resist as much by the second round. I was on to them. They asked me to participate and do it the other way around. Start with the negative self-talk statements. So I did. Surprisingly, my arm couldn't resist the negative words; as much as I tried to fight against them, I couldn't resist. After all, the person pressing on my arm was a big, tall man, and clearly gravity and testosterone and muscles were at play here, too. Not fair.

For three full minutes, I tried to resist. I fatigued my arm and pushed against the force of the opposition as much as I could. But I sure didn't do it very effectively. By the end, my arm felt like lead. Then, they asked me to do it again, immediately, with my arm as heavy as concrete, but to stand tall, plant my feet on the ground, and say my positive affirmations. With full doubt at the ready, I was eager to show them how wrong they were. I held firm; the large man pushed against me, and I started: "I am strong! I can resist! I am a leader! I am powerful! I can do anything!" To my amazement, as tired as my arm was, it was immovable. I started yelling the affirmations, "I've got this! I am as strong as a boulder! I am powerful!" My arm didn't move. The words that came out of my mouth were true—both times. I am weak. I can't do this. I'm not enough. True. But then immediately: I can do this. I am strong. I am powerful. Also true. If you don't believe me, try it. Right now. Grab a buddy and try it.

The Power Of Words

Ever since that day over twenty years ago, I believe in the power of my words. Of your words. Whatever I tell myself about myself is reflected in my worth and my value and how that shows up in my life. Sure, it's still a battle, but even if I don't quite believe something yet, I have to hold on to the possibility that it's true. You've got to believe in yourself to do this work. I believe in you. I believe in you a lot, actually—but sadly, that's not enough. So, reader, I am intentionally inviting you into this work, too. Join me in believing in you. Join me in believing in your worth and value, your joys and creativity, your boldness and quiet strength. Right now, just as you are. You are amazing. You are enough. You are a counselor. You are doing it. You can. You will. You are. Not after you finish your internship. Not after you get your degree finished. Not once you get licensed. Not once you have a full caseload. Not after whatever bar you have for yourself that says, "When I get _____, then I'll have arrived." Nope, not then. Here and now.

Once you start speaking your positive affirmations and speaking truth to your value and your worth, your arms, your body, and your being will begin to believe it. Your head will believe it. *Your heart will believe it.* You will see that the heart of counseling is really all about you, your worth, your value, and your brilliance. Right here and right now. Just as you are. Your positive beliefs about you will start weaving into the cracks in your heart that the ghosts left.

And it's time, counselors, to start living in the space of your positive beliefs about who you are at your core. It's time to take that space of believing you are worthy, skilled, brilliant, strong, and resilient. That your spicy self and your fierceness and your softness and your tentative self and your confident self and your introverted and extroverted and your Enneagram[2] 1-9 self is enough. Because of the work of our ghosts, we have some battling to do in order to believe these things that are true about ourselves. And while they are already true, sometimes it takes practice to believe them. It's an intention. Grab my hand, and let's go. Let's walk together into the space where I practice my self-affirmations and you practice your self-affirmations, and side by side we stand as completely different people, but each with a core part of us that is wholly and fully enough.

Create Your Fight Song

As we walk together, I encourage you to find the words—your words—to help you fight. Fight to see the good, the brilliance in you. I invite you to create a fight song. Maybe it's not, "I am strong. I am powerful. I will resist," like in the leadership activity. Or maybe it is.

A fight song creates a strong shield inside us, one that deflects the attempts at comparison or imposter syndrome. The song keeps the ghosts at bay. It reminds us of our worth. An everyday fight song. Not just for the days when the ghosts stampede in, but for all the days, all the sessions, the "worst session ever" days and the "that session was fine" days and the "I'm the best counselor ever" days. Yes, there will be those days, too. And those days are incredibly important. Savor them. Honor them. Share about them and write about them. Let those sink into those deep spaces in your heart. Let those move into the middle, core space of your heart just as much (or more!) than "the worst session ever" days. Give those "I'm the best counselor ever" days a voice, too. Those help solidify your fight song.

Let me make a caveat here: this fight song is not "Keep fighting. Keep going. Keep going when the storm comes. Keep going when your heart breaks. Keep going when the world feels dark. Finish grad school no matter what." Nope. It's not the "Pull yourself up by your bootstraps" bullshit. That's not the fight song I'm talking about. Pushing, doing, and achieving until the point of exhaustion is NOT the fight song here. This fight song is the fight for your worth. Your value. Right here as you are. This fight song includes positive affirmations and healthy self-talk and is filled with love, with listening within, and with compassion. For you. That's the fight song right there. The one that wraps its arms around you and says, "I see you. And you're good. You are so good."

After that awful-terrible-no-good session that I referenced earlier, the one where I was convinced I was both too much and not enough, I cried. My fears and doubts flooded my head and my heart. And reader, if that happens to you, please know it's okay and super normal. It's okay to feel overcome with heavy emotions about our work, and it's okay if that sometimes seeps into our worth as well. This fight song, though, is one you call upon during those moments so a moment doesn't turn into several days or a month or a semester or a lifetime.

After that session, I called upon my fight song. A fight song to battle my specific brand of negative self-talk, which is all around being too much and not enough. And when I call on my fight song, it looks a bit like this:

You are enough. *You* are enough. You *are* enough. You are ***enough***.

You are strong enough. Smart enough. Capable enough. Sensitive enough.

I'm okay. I am so very okay.

> Because the room isn't empty at all—I'm there. My heart is there. My head is there. And words that I speak become true.

And I spoke these words. Out loud to the empty room. Because the room wasn't empty at all—I was there. My heart was there. My head was there. And the words that I spoke became true.

These words have power. They shape my reality, and I want my reality to communicate my value and my worth.

When these affirmations, like in this case, are specific to my work as a counselor, I add statements like:

You are doing what you are called to do. And you are *good at it.* You are called to pour into others, help them see their truths, help them fight the lies, and help them move through their trauma. And sometimes that work is hard. And just because it doesn't feel good doesn't mean this isn't good work.

Worth The Fight

Your positive affirmations, your fight song, likely look different than my fight song. And so, reader, it's time to create your own fight song. For when it feels heavy and exhausting. A fight song for when it feels like pure joy, and for when you want to quit, and for when you want to savor all the things. A fight song for when you get lost in the sea of "I can't do this" and "I suck." And a fight song when you begin to discover or rediscover that you love this work, that it brings you joy and purpose and direction. A fight song for you. About you. In honor of you. And such a beautiful gift for you.

There are no rules about this fight song, no boundaries, no expectations. You don't have to share it or write it down or prove its worth to anyone. This assignment is not graded; it's not even pass or fail. Your fight song is brilliant because it's for you. It is a love letter to yourself that reminds you of your worth and your value that already exists in that amazing human body of yours. The fight song that resists the push against. Please begin to create it, write it, dream it, ponder it. I invite you to begin the creative writing of your own fight song. It can be one line or one word. It can build over time. You can use mine or parts of mine and claim it as yours. It's your fight song because you are worth the fight. You always have been, and you always will be.

You are irreplaceable. Priceless. You have gifts that nobody else has, which are so special to you and so special for others. You are captivating. You carry a brilliant spark inside you that nobody else carries. It's your spark, and the world needs it. You are unique and beautiful and your true self, your authentic self. You are just right just the way you are. You are already worthy. You are already enough. Your desire (and fear) to be seen and deeply known is tender and deserving. I want you to believe it. I want you to know that your body, breath, soul, and every ounce of who you are is not too much or not enough of anything. And that who you are is your greatest gift.

CHAPTER FOURTEEN

Rooted

W e drove down Sunset Highway, surrounded by rolling hills of fir trees reaching tall around us, headed to the Oregon coast. The shade of these trees provided a glimpse into the cooler temperatures we sought from the coastal breezes on a particularly hot day in Portland. We drove for miles, sheltered by these old, solid trees.

As we drove, we passed signs that read:
Planted 2006
Planted 2012
Planted 2021

Acres of once-barren land from trees being harvested, planted with new saplings that had grown into trees of varying heights, but growing, almost looking eager to join the tall shade trees providing cooler air to the travelers on the highway. My mind wandered to the idea of growth, of stretching, of reaching toward the sun and blue skies. I could almost feel my body rising on the seat of the car, straightening, wishing for the sunshine that I knew was right above the trees. The trees grew so straight, with such determination, such fortitude, such ease. I wondered how they so effortlessly grew straight up towards the sky while my own growth seems to zig and zag and take such drastic turns and curves sometimes. I wondered what my own growth would look like in a tree.

As we drove, my heart swelled with connections between myself and the earth, sometimes quite different and sometimes quite similar. I saw the fallen trees, almost melting into the soil below, providing nutrients and purpose to the trees still standing. My heart drifted to the legacy of love of those who have gone before us who do the same for us: give us purpose and direction as they nurture, as they step aside to let us grow and become. I saw the ferns, ivy, and moss as part of the ground cover below, growing purely because of the shade of the taller trees. My heart felt thankful for the shade and direction of the tall trees, providing me shelter to grow and learn and spread across the earth.

As we continued to drive, suddenly the skies opened, and the sunshine spread across the highway before us. To our left and to our right was expansive openness. We passed another sign that read:

Planted 2023

That's this year. The acres and acres that spread before us were filled with saplings planted in the last six months. They stood no more than a foot tall, and no taller trees were around to shade them from the sunshine.

I felt relieved that the sunshine was so accessible to them. But gosh, they were so little. I wondered how tall they would grow before the darkness of the Oregon rain would come. I wondered how these little saplings could make it through the cold of the impending winter without the protection of the larger, sturdier trees. My heart almost ached for them. Who planted these, so young and little, out here in the middle of nowhere? Shouldn't they be bigger before being transplanted out here? I wondered so much about this for the trees and for us, as beginners, as newly planted counselors. I wondered how on earth little plants could grow in a cold and dark land.

Below The Surface

And then I remembered that what my eyes can see is only part of the story. It's only part of the full truth of what is happening with this little tree. Because below the surface of the earth is a whole other story. Below, in the soil, the story is unfolding and spreading and growing—maybe not taller right now, but deeper. The rows and rows of tiny little trees stretched deep into the earth below, beyond the space where our sight could capture.

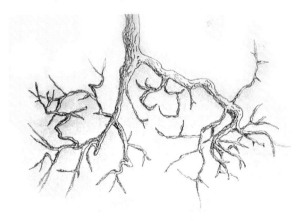

These trees are a lot like us. Our growth as humans, as parents, as partners, as friends, as counselors begins underground, where nobody else sees. It starts in the dirt, in the decay, in the dying, in the depths of the protected. Our growth starts, for many of us, because of the hurts and pains and darkness. It's where the work that nobody sees begins.

Before you picked up this book or applied for a graduate counseling program or before you signed up for classes, your roots were growing and spreading, sometimes down below, where nobody else could see. Where your flight of song could not be traced by even the keenest of eyes. Where the harshness of weather or words won't knock us down. Where the heat of the sun or the pressure from humans won't make us wilt into nothing. Before I could see the growth of the saplings spread across the earth before me, they grew deep into the ground. The roots spread through the soil. Your growth, the sprouts that are being nurtured by the sun and rain, were growing under the surface, too. Your growth to becoming a counselor started long before this moment. Those roots were growing. And it's those roots that brought you here.

> Your growth, the sprouts that are being nurtured by the sun and rain, were growing under the surface, too. Your growth to becoming a counselor started long before this moment. Those roots were growing. And it's those roots that brought you here.

Are You A Counselor?

I had a professor in my master's degree program who knew of things below the surface that cannot be seen. That we had already been planted. That you have already been planted. Our roots are already growing deeper before we emerge into the light. It was my Introduction to Counseling class. The first time I gathered my organized binders and printed syllabi and color-coded highlighters ready to use. The class where I felt like everyone was staring at me, wondering why I was there. But also a tiny sense that maybe I did belong there (but also with a healthy dose of maybe I didn't).

He had us introduce ourselves. He started in the back of the room and told us to zigzag up the rows until we had all gone. Darn it, that meant I went second. The person sitting next to me went first. I didn't know them. They said their name, their specific program, and what they wanted to learn from the class.

I felt myself sweating. I didn't even really hear their name because I wanted to make sure I remembered my own. After they went, I was ready to jump in and get this over with. I'm a confident introvert, and doing these introductions to a classroom full of people was my nightmare. Before I could jump in, the professor asked the first student, "And are you a counselor?" Ummm...what? Clearly, no. Holy crap, what was this special kind of hell? The classmate slowly turned to me with a look of confusion and panic in their eyes. The classmate tentatively responded, "Well, no, not yet. That's why I'm here." I looked back at them and tried to communicate with my eyes that I had no idea and that seemed like a perfect answer to me.

The professor softly and encouragingly waited. The student continued, "This is my first class ever, so no, I'm not a counselor yet." The professor, who had been sitting on the table in the front, approached the student in the back with a warm smile on his face, extended his hand to the student, and, shaking their hand, said, "You're already a counselor, Chris. Welcome to class." Then he shared with us, almost with a hushed voice, that coming to class and reading the books and completing all of the assignments wasn't going to make us a counselor. We already were. Our roots were already growing deep into the soil of becoming, and now it was time to belong in this space as a counselor.

It was my turn. I shared my name and program, then looked at him with great anticipation. What was next? Was I supposed to say anything? The professor said, "And you are a...." I looked at the professor and, with a questioning voice, said, "Counselor?" "Yes!" He smiled, and his face looked delighted. "You are Michelle, and you are a counselor." I then replied, "I am Michelle, and I am a counselor." He responded, "You are a counselor, Michelle. Welcome to class. You belong here."

He continued around the room, and as people caught on, they began to share the space by saying, "I'm Tasha, and I'm a counselor," "I'm Liz, and I'm a counselor." After each person would share that, the professor would say one more thing:

You are a counselor, Nic. *You belong here.*
You are a counselor, Dana. *There's room for you here.*
You are a counselor, Maria. *You're growing already.*
You are a counselor, Dani. *The world needs you.*
You are a counselor, Nancy. *You are rooted.*
You are a counselor, Jessica. *You've already been planted.*
You are a counselor, Brandon. *I can't wait to see your fruit.*
You are a counselor, Sherri. *You have great purpose.*

You are valued. You are needed. Your calling on your life matters. You belong. There's room for you in the profession. There's great need for you in this profession. You are created to be here. I'm so thankful you are here. You are needed. You are special. The world needs you. I see you growing already. I believe in you. Your growth matters.

Reader, the same is true for you. If I could sit with you and look at you—really look at you—I would share these words with you. I would fully welcome you to the profession of counseling. I would let you know *you belong here.* I would tell you through a hushed voice and with so much intent and meaning that *there's room for you here.* I would share with you, for the first time or the hundredth time, that *you have great purpose*, *you are rooted*, and *the world needs you.*

You Are A Counselor

Dear reader, it's time I stop calling you a dear reader (although you are exactly that as well) and call you what you are, dear counselor. Dear counselor, you belong here. Dear counselor, there's room for you here. Dear counselor, the world needs you. Dear counselor, you have a great purpose. Dear counselor, I'm so thankful you are here. Your roots are growing and spreading and growing deeper. And while the small sapling growing above the surface might not show your growth yet, it doesn't mean it's not there. You have already been planted, counselor. You are already growing. Your roots are already growing deeper.

Like the student who went before me in class who respond- ed, "Well, no, not yet. That's why I'm here," many of us sit wait- ing to be. Hoping. Questioning if we ever will be. Waiting for the education to make us a counselor or writing fifty papers to make us a counselor. Maybe, just maybe, counselor, *you already are.* You are already built for it. You are already made for it. It's already growing inside you, deep below the surface, where the soil is ripe and warm. Your roots are deepening into the soil that represents who you are and what you want to become. The roots are inviting you, surrounding you, reminding you. You are planted. You belong here. Right here, counselor. You belong.

Dear counselor, I'm so thankful you are here. Your roots are growing and spreading and growing deeper.

The beautiful thing about our roots, the work happening underground, is they serve incredibly important functions to the health of the tree. The roots you are already growing beneath the surface are already protecting you. Being rooted, feeling like you belong, being here is actually more important than the fruit you produce. Both are important and essential, but you cannot have the top of the tree without the beginning, the creation, the rootedness of the tree. Because you see, counselor, the roots of the tree are where the health and stability of the tree come from.

Weather The Storms

Living in the Pacific Northwest, we've had our share of difficult weather that has challenged the growth and stability of our beautiful trees. A few years ago, a terrible ice storm froze boughs and branches, and many trees broke off at various levels. In one terrible, overnight, heavy ice storm, our neighborhood lost hundreds of trees.

As we walked through the deafening silence the morning after, we saw skeletons of trees, the ground covered in brokenness. But as I looked around that morning, my eyes could only see part of the story. My eyes could not see the depths of the heart of the tree. My eyes could only see part of the tree. Like the drive along Sunset Highway among the tall, strong fir trees and the small, seemingly frail fir trees, what my eyes could see was only part of the picture. The seeming value of the shade of the tree or the nutrients of the fallen trees or the cool, damp soil the tree provided for other ground cover isn't the whole story.

Just like when you wrote your "I am" statements in chapter three or when I ask students to do this exercise during class on the whiteboard. It's only part of the story. Because, dear counselor, the growth, the protection, the expansive green of the aboveground part is a *mirror reflection of the roots*. It exists because of the growth underneath. You are like this, too. Your root system is a beautiful and essential foundation that provides the mirrored reflection of what we produce when we are dwelling in the deep. When we are planted. When we belong.

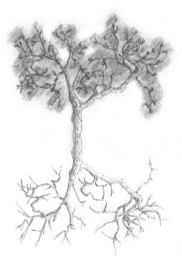

Counselors, our root systems, our purpose, our belonging are so important to help us weather storms, to help us fight against heat and pressure. For us to grow tall and produce flowers and fruit, to identify our "I am" statements, we have to be rooted and know our purpose: our living and nurturing and healing purpose. I've had many storms in my time as a counselor and as a professor—more than I wish to count. Sometimes my leaves turned yellow. Sometimes I stopped growing for a season. Sometimes my leaves turned crunchy and brown. But with my roots growing deep into the soil, I remained. My sense of purpose and belonging and my calling to grow here helped me stay anchored.

And, counselor, you are already growing roots. As my professor demonstrated, you and I are already planted and growing and taking root. And your roots are already producing mirror reflections above ground as your branches grow and your buds open. You are a counselor. You're not waiting to be; you already are. Sometimes the reminders are important, though. I was sharing some recent struggles with a colleague about work, and he, with love, said, "Why do you stay, then?" I took a great pause. It's easy to get wrapped up in the drama and the insecurities. When faced with that question, I had an answer. It was buried and burdened, but I had an answer deep down in my root system. When I allowed my roots to reflect what I wanted my branches and boughs to bear, it was congruent. It gave me permission to let my growth be a mirror image of my roots, my purpose, my depths. Counselor, what is your answer? What are the words that exist deep within you? What are the root systems that help you produce the fruit and growth at the top of the tree?

Grow Deep

This is my great wish for you, dear counselor. My wish is that your roots grow deep, your purpose is clarified, and your sense of belonging is watered so that you can grow and bear fruit. My hope is that you dwell in the deep. That your roots grow so deeply below the surface that you are able to grow and do what you are shaped for. That the deep work below the surface provides a reflection of what grows above. You are meant to be here because of who you are, not despite it. My longing is that you would go out there and fill the space where you are called. The below-the-surface spaces and the above-ground spaces, like a tree growing towards, up, out, and across. That you would believe, deep down in the darkness of the soil below, that you have something beautiful to offer. And it's time, dear counselor, that you grow fruits that reflect the depths of growth below the surface of your authentic self. The world needs you. You belong here, dear counselor.

> The deep work below the surface provides a reflection of what grows above. You are meant to be here because of who you are, not despite it.

You are valued. You are needed. Your calling on your life matters. You belong. There's room for you in the profession. There's great need for you in this profession. You are created to be here. I'm so thankful you are here. You are needed. You are special. The world needs you. I see you growing already. I believe in you. Your growth matters.

Just like my professor said to me over twenty years ago, you are a counselor. You belong here.

CHAPTER FIFTEEN

Dear Counselor

S ometimes I hear things from clients that make me cringe. Clients come in and share words I've shared that have really impacted them, and sometimes they're brilliant, and I think to myself, "I'm pretty sure I didn't say that, but it's brilliant!" Or other times, I think, "That's asinine—surely I didn't say anything like that!" I don't know if they came from other well-meaning professionals or if the words got filtered and understood differently than they were intended, because both are likely true sometimes.

The same thing happens as a professor. Sometimes it's my own words students repeat back to me, and I think to myself, "There's no way I said that." One of the things I hear quite a bit from students that makes me cringe is this encouragement for beginning counselors (or experienced ones, for that matter) to take off their "mom" hat or their "friend" hat or their "husband" hat when they are in the counseling room and put on their "counselor" hat. I get the intent behind the suggestion, but I think it's short-sighted and complete garbage.

Dear Counselor, Wear Your Hats

To demonstrate this, one day in class, I brought all my daughter's hats in from home. She was well into the make-believe stage during that season, so I had a good assortment. I had a police hat, crown, firefighter hat, cowboy hat, witch hat, sun visor, cat ears, astronaut helmet, superhero hat, beach hat, running hat, pirate hat...you get the idea. I brought all these hats to class and walked in the door with all of them stacked one on top of another on my head. They were hard to balance, and sometimes I dropped one or two, which added to the reality and metaphor of the exercise.

What I shared with the students is that we cannot remove our "mom" hat or our "brother" hat or our "accountant" hats when we sit with clients. When I go into the counseling room, I have an inability to not think about my daughter's school presentation on Sacagawea today or her field trip and her nerves about riding the bus. I can't *not* think about the testing my mom was having for her breast cancer or the job interview my husband had that day.

We are human, and these relationships and these roles and these "hats" that we wear are an important part of our identity. They make us whole. They make you who you are. They help you connect with others deeply in ways our "therapist" hat cannot. Because let's be honest, that therapist hat is filled with tasks and to-do's and questions and interventions and education. It's the other hats that you wear that actually give your therapist hat meaning, that give it a place to land. It's all the other hats you wear, the identities you have, that bring empathy and compassion and validation and comfort and joy to the work of being a counselor. Our other identities are part of what helps bring us to the heart of this work as a counselor.

My encouragement to you is rather than trying to take off these various hats and set them aside for our work as a counselor, that you work to rearrange the landscape of the hats when you sit in the office with clients. Trying to keep your therapist hat on and only your therapist hat is incredibly exhausting. It's exhausting work to try to keep out all the other parts of us in our work as counselors. And, honestly, that's the place where counselors go to die. Where they burn out, hate their work, and eventually quit their job. It starts in the place of trying to keep our other hats off completely. Keeping out the other parts of you when you're in the room as a counselor prevents you from accessing the heart space, the parts of you that connect, nurture, support, love, and hold space.

Keeping out those other identities encourages you to remain in your head and thinking space. When you allow *you* in, your feelings, your authenticity, your vulnerability, and your heart come, too. And when you bring your heart into the room, that's where the brilliant and beautiful work of counseling and connection happens. Because you are so brilliant and beautiful, and all of your identities along the way have helped make you fully you. Please, dear counselor, invite those pieces of you in—all of them. Those identities help you be brave, help you be curious, help you wonder and care and focus and get distracted and show up fully human.

I do my very best to make sure my "counselor" hat is *on the top* when I'm in the counseling room (and frankly, it's not always possible). When I'm teaching, I do my very best to make sure my "teacher" hat is on top and the guiding identity in the room. But what makes us brilliantly unique is *the very nature of our hats*. My mom hat, my wife hat, my teacher hat, my daughter hat, my coach hat, my runner hat—they all bring certain characteristics that make me *me*.

217

My mom hat helps me be compassionate and forgiving and playful. My wife hat helps me be empathetic, my teacher hat helps me slow down and be a lifelong learner. They all have great metaphors for how they inform our work and how we show up as a full human being with our clients. Your clients don't want some robotic, mechanical, theory-driven, role-play rehearsed version of you. They want the full you. Dear counselor, wear your hats. Clients want the you who tears up with them more than the books say is appropriate when they share about having another miscarriage. They want the full you who laughs at a story the client is sharing before you realize you're "supposed to" filter those laughs and make sure they're appropriate. They want the you who is both honest and professional when they ask, "How are you?" They want the you who will go completely off track only to find something that is relevant at the end of the rabbit trail that can only be found by being flexible and curious and trusting yourself. Please, dear counselor, wear your hats. They make you beautifully and authentically you.

Dear Counselor, Be You

Sometimes we are authentically ourselves, whether we intend to be or not. I was doing a telehealth session with a couple. I was in my home office, and they were in their home, sitting on a futon couch in their guest room. They had come into counseling several months prior, after the discovery of infidelity in their marriage. We had done a lot of deep and excruciating work. They were dedicated to creating a healthy marriage and repairing the many layers of damage, pain, and lies that had occurred. And this couple had shown up each week and were doing the hard work. We were talking about a specific aspect of trust. They were turned towards one another, holding hands and sharing their hearts, through tears. It was a beautiful and touching moment. One that required me to remain mostly quiet and let them do the intimate work they had sought so hard to do.

All of a sudden, less than six inches behind my computer on the wall crawled the biggest, nastiest spider ever. The kind with hairy, wide legs and a big, hairy body. The kind where if you suck it up a vacuum, it makes a thumping noise. The kind of spider that, when my husband sees it, he gets a little yucked out, too. And just for the record, I am not one of those people who loves spiders or captures them to release them outside. I'm one of those people who screams for my husband to rescue me from great distress when there's a spider anywhere near me. I'm the person who won't even smack it with a shoe because it requires me to get much closer to the spider than I want to get, and it might scurry as I approach and crawl right up my pant leg and I might die. And no, we don't have poisonous spiders where we live. There it crawled, slowly up the wall, just inches from my laptop.

What on earth was I supposed to do? I'm far too professional (ha!) to scream. I'm far too poised (ha!) to freak out. Also, I'm far too scared to just sit there! I'm far too wimpy to let it crawl up the rest of the wall!

So, what did I do? I screamed. I yelled, without any forethought, "Oh my gosh, there's a huge spider!" The wife stood up screaming, thinking I saw one in her space. She was dancing around, screaming, and I joined her. There we were, two strong and successful women, dancing around our spaces, running from a spider. The moment of tenderness had clearly passed.

Once she learned it was in my house, not hers, she started coaxing me on, providing encouragement to face the spider.

I grabbed my computer and turned the camera to show her this gargantuan spider, to which the husband's eyes lit up, and he muttered, "Oh, that's nasty. Even I would run from that thing." The next few minutes, they encouraged me to grab a book and toss it at the spider. Eventually, I did. The spider died a quick death all over my wall, and we all settled down.

The laughter, shared experience, and slight role reversal provided such groundwork for talking about fears. I admitted I had a fear of spiders, apologized for my lack of professionalism, and they shared how reassuring it was for them to see me being me. The wife shared that sometimes it felt really vulnerable to share her fears with someone who seemed so "put together." I laughed. But the conversation that happened was one of vulnerability, honesty, and truth. I showed up. Fully me.

We talked about how much she fears this mask of perfection she wears and how it prevents them from really talking about their struggles. They talked about how much she's holding back her authentic self when people ask her how she's doing and they don't know about the pain of the affair. And she shared how honest she wants to be with them but feels she can't be fully honest. The "I'm a professional woman in the community" hat was always on top, never making room for her "and I'm broken, too" hat and her "I'm lonely" hat and her "I need help" hat. She left that session feeling convicted to let others know they were in couples counseling, hoping this step had started to take down the wall she had built up, hiding her full self from others. She shared that she felt nudged to share because I let her see me. I let her see my fear, my ridiculous spider dance, my messy room behind the well-organized telehealth view. And when she did, it helped her realize there's more to me than what she saw, and there's more to her than what others see, too. And that maybe allowing others to see more of her was brave and vulnerable and an important part of her that deserved to be shared with others.

> And your fullness is exactly what your clients need. It helps you relate to people in ways I cannot, in ways your colleagues cannot.

All of these hats that we wear, that you wear, counselor, have created the amazing, beautiful you. And, contrary to what you might hear in your graduate program or from your professors or colleagues, let me encourage you to wear all your hats. Please don't try to take off your mom hat as a counselor. Please don't try to take off your motorcycle-driving-tattoo-loving hat as a counselor. It's what makes you fully you. And your fullness is exactly what your clients need. It helps you relate to people in ways I cannot, in ways your colleagues cannot. And being fully, authentically you includes the parts we are proud to show and the parts that feel more vulnerable for us to show. While we might not share with our clients the parts of ourselves that the ghosts meddle around with, those parts help us be present with clients in really important ways. Our brokenness helps us see those areas of brokenness, need, and longing in other people, too.

Dear Counselor, Your Story Matters

Brokenness can show up in beautiful, unexpected ways. Several years ago, our family visited an indoor butterfly garden. Our daughter, little at the time, was enamored with the butterflies flying around, their wings fluttering so close to us and some-times ever so lightly landing on us. As a nature-loving family, my daughter had learned how fragile and delicate butterfly wings can be and how even touching them takes off the scales from their wings. As we walked around in awe of the butterflies, one landed right on her small arm. This butterfly, though, looked like it had escaped being eaten by a bird. Part of two wings were gone, leaving jagged edges. My daughter was awestruck by this butterfly. More than the rest. More than the perfectly shaped butterflies flying all around her. She was drawn to the brokenness and unwavering beauty of this one, the one that was tattered and worn.

And we are like this, too. Our broken, tattered wings are a beautiful part of our story, of our flight, of our uniqueness. They tell a tale of wisdom, learning, growing, bravery, pain, suf-fering, and redemption. And those are important parts of our story, indeed. When clients experience us, fully us, it gives them permission to take a look, to wonder, and to think that maybe they are beautiful and unique just the way they are, too: broken, battered, torn, and worn. Wholeness doesn't mean without bro-kenness. Counselor doesn't mean without the fullness of you. And counselor, it is brave for you to show up in those spaces—broken, battered wings and all.

Sometimes, that brokenness and batteredness is evident, and we wear it like a tattoo; it has created who we are. And sometimes it's underneath, where it's safe and protected. The invitation is not to show clients all of our hats, not to invite them to coffee or tell them your life story from the perspective of each of the hats, but to let the hats inform how we show up with our clients. How we access the empathy and compassion needed to serve them well as a counselor. And counselor, when you allow your stories and identities to serve as a lifeline to connect with others, that is brave.

Dear Counselor, Be Brave

Wearing your hats and being your authentic self is brave. Showing clients your spider-fearing self is brave. We tend to think of being brave as big bravery, doing something huge and out of the box and big, bold and risk-taking. I think bravery in counseling (and in life, frankly) is much more about little bravery. It's being a little preoccupied with your other hats because those hats matter. It's the day-to-day, seemingly mundane things we do multiple times a day that make us brave.

Little bravery is about showing up for ourselves and others in ways that might otherwise go unnoticed. Little bravery is huge, dear counselor. It matters. It is meaningful. It helps me make scary things just a little bit less scary. It paves the way to making important decisions that move us in the direction of growth and change in small, important, meaningful ways. It's the little bravery that shows up when you call your teen client's parent for the first time. Or when you walk into your supervisor's office and say you're stuck or overwhelmed or confused or triggered. You are brave when you leave the office on time. And when you carve out a short break in your day. Little bravery is when you wake up fifteen minutes early to do a meditation exercise, when you finally end a session on time, or when you ask for that extension on the paper. The little bravery matters. Every single day, those little braveries add up to amazing change and progress and growth.

When I teach practicum and internship classes, I sit with those of you who are about to sit with your first-ever "real" client. As you learn the agency policies and paperwork, excitement builds as your first client draws near. During those first few weeks of class and in the weeks that follow, finding, seeking, and stating your little bravery matters. It matters, counselor. The ways in which you show up with little bravery matter so much. As I introduce myself to the class, I simply share, "I want to see you be brave." I ask each student to share how they've been brave this week. And I'm talking about the little bravery. You don't even need a list—just one thing. One way in which you've been brave this week. For me, today, I was brave when I remembered to take my vitamins. I was brave when I took the shortest of walks during my thirty-minute break and enjoyed the fresh air. I was brave when I shared with a colleague that I got triggered during a session and stopped listening for a few short minutes. The little bravery matters.

Counselor, how have *you* been brave this week? Can you shuttle down to your heart and feel for the little things that actually felt quite big and meaningful to you? How did you show up with little bravery this week? What are the seemingly insignificant things that, when you speak them or put words to them, matter just a little bit more?

Here's the beautiful thing that happens in class when I ask students to share their little bravery. They shrug it off at first. They say things like, "I didn't do anything brave," or "I just did the regular counselor things," or "I was far more scared than brave this week." But then, just one person, one of you out there, digs deep into your vulnerability bank and shares. And this very act is brave. Incredibly brave, actually. You share just one little thing that felt brave. You share things like:

I didn't quit/run away/scream/crawl under the rug.
I invited a client's partner in for couples counseling.
I charged a client for a late cancellation.
I actually had fun with a client.
I got to my internship site without using a GPS.
I wrote my first progress note.
I asked a client to sign the video release form.

Yes! Those things are so brave, dear counselor. So brave. And you did those things! You showed up, and you were incredibly brave. What happens is that sharing your little bravery gives others permission to share their bravery, too. It changes how people think about what it means to be brave, what it means to show up, and it changes the meaning of what bravery is really all about. And then, tears come. Students cry. Because it's hard and scary to be a beginning counselor. Everything is new and different and strange and scary. And then when we are asked to think about how we navigate through those things, we begin to see just how many things we do every single day that are brave. Every single day, you are navigating new territory and trying new things and learning new steps and discovering new parts of you. You are showing up fully you, or moving in the direction of learning how to be. And that is so brave. Dear counselor, you are so brave.

It is so brave to see the small things we do each and every day to move us toward growing deeper and more fruitful as a counselor. The ways we extend our roots deeper and our branches taller. The field of counseling is a quiet and private profession. You have to care about the work you do because nobody is going to see your wins. The nature of the profession is that nobody sees when we're brave; nobody feels what it feels like in your body when you have a really amazing session. Sure, sometimes clients are in that process with us, but nobody will acknowledge our bravery, our wins, our warm fuzzy sessions. It's up to you. It's up to you to see your little bravery.

Dear Counselor, Thank You

As I come to the end of this journey with you in these pages, it feels honoring to end our time together like I have done before with groups of amazing counselors. It's not quite the same because I can't see you. I can't feel you. I can't hear your joys and your celebrations and your fears and your struggles with your ghosts or imposter syndrome. But I have traveled this road with so many just like you. Today, let's close our time together with a thank you letter. A thank you letter to you. There are no rules or boundaries or expectations for this letter. It's yours. For you, about you, celebrating you, giving thanksgiving for the ways you show up as a counselor. And counselor, there are so many ways. Take your time; give yourself space and processing and feeling time. Sink into your heart and give yourself permission to be thankful for all the ways you show up for yourself.

Some brave counselors who have gone before you shared parts of their thank you letters. I share these with humility for the trust, with thanksgiving for the vulnerability, and with sincere appreciation and admiration for the honesty and transparency. Counselors, you are brave in all the ways you are showing up for you. And these are the words you've shared with me, with the readers of this book, and with yourself.

Dear counselor,

Thank you for sharing your love and light with the world. It needs you.

Thank you for staying curious, even though it can be hard work.

Thank you for staying soft and tender.

Thank you for considering multiple perspectives, even when you think you're right.

Thank you for giving vigilance a time slot on the day calendar.

Thank you for being courageous.

Thank you for going through with it, even though you were so nervous to do the session.

Thank you for getting out of bed.

Thank you for breathing.

Thank you for listening to my needs.

Thank you for taking your meds.

Thank you for your willingness.

Thank you for showing up and doing the work.

Thank you for the work you're doing to learn who you are as a therapist, even as you admire others and how they do things.

Thank you for not letting the thing you don't know stop you from sharing the things you do.

Thank you for knowing you are enough even when you feel like you aren't.

Dear counselor, write your own thank you letter to you. Take time to appreciate, acknowledge, and see what you are doing today, this week, and this month to be brave. And write it down. Just start. Dear counselor, thank you for...

My Thank You To You, Dear Counselor

Dear counselor, this book, these words, have been an act of love and obedience from start to finish. I hope you feel the love, compassion, and care in my words. While attachment cannot be created solely through a book like it can from one human to another human, my hope is that these words have been a source of light, life, compassion, and a deep sense of knowing, of being seen. My hope is that these words will serve as a guide for you in your journey to becoming more fully you each and every day. Because you matter so deeply. Your heart matters in this work. I desperately desire these words to reach into the deepest parts of you needing to be loved in extraordinary ways. You were made for this. You can do this. You are brilliant and beautiful and created for this work.

Some days, my job is hard, but today is not one of them. I am honored to have been a small part of your journey and I will continue to stand along the pathway and be your cheerleader as you pave ahead into what's next. Thank you for doing this work. Thank you for committing to this field. Thank you for signing up to do this work for the long haul. Thank you for sitting with the brokenhearted. Thank you for living out your purpose. Thank you for your bravery, commitment, perseverance, authenticity, and vulnerability. Thank you for showing up fully you. Thank you for your commitment to your heart and the heart of this work. Thank you, deeply and sincerely, for doing the work, the work of the heart of counseling.

> Thank you for showing up fully you. Thank you for your commitment to your heart and the heart of this work. Thank you, deeply and sincerely, for doing the work, the work of the heart of counseling.

ACKNOWLEDGEMENTS

My Heart People

A t the beginning of each year, I pick a word (or the word/wand picks me) and I apply that to my life for the full year. This year, two words emerged: *walk* and *savor*. I prayed over and contemplated these words. What did they mean? What would they reveal? And why two words this year? And then, a friend gave me a third word: *create*. Those words started my year just eight short months ago.

Walk
Savor
Create

And boy, did I. I wondered for several days what I might create. For a few months, I had been kicking around the idea of writing a book. Surely that wasn't it. I wasn't ready. So what was I to create instead? A few days later, I got an email from Hope*Media, inviting me (and their whole email subscriber list, I'm sure) to submit an application to write a book. That night, Adam was making dinner, and with a glass of wine in hand, I sat at the counter while he cooked, and I filled out that application and hit the send button.

A few weeks later, I got the email. "Congratulations," it read. What? For real? I could write an actual book? Crap, now what? I wasn't really serious about it; I was just kicking around the idea. Adam and I went for a silent prayer walk together. We walked (my word!), and we prayed; we walked, and we prayed. Silently yet together. At the front steps, we paused, and I said, "Did you hear anything?" and he tentatively said, "Not much, just a phrase." Me too! I said, "Just a short phrase, over and over again." That short phrase we heard? It was the same exact phrase: "This is what's next." That night, I signed the contract, and I've been creating, savoring, and walking ever since.

Adam, you have been with me on this journey since the words "This is what's next" came out of our mouths. You've wiped tears; you've celebrated every single completed chapter. Thank you for struggling through it with me to lessen the burden I felt. Thank you for always encouraging me to dig deeper, to stay in the depths, to write through tears, and to stick to my schedule. I know it's cliche to say I couldn't have done this without you, but it's a true and deep fact. Without you, there would be no book. You are my co-author in many ways. You are so deeply precious to me. Thank you for loving me in all the ways you do. I love you.

Claire, my sweet and spunky daughter. You were behind me all the way. Before I signed on the dotted line, we talked with you about sacrifice and dedication and what it might mean for me to write a book. You jumped for joy when it was time to celebrate and hugged me when you knew I was stuck. You showed up for me and in the words of this book in profound ways. Thank you for always showing me how to keep growing and learning and for teaching me so much along the way. I am so proud of you, and I am so thankful to be your mommy. You and Dad are my most favorite people ever. You inspire me. You encourage me. I love you so much.

The idea of this book was like a seed that could not have grown without first being planted, becoming rooted, and blooming. Thank you to those of you who provided a nourishing field in which to grow.

Thank you to my parents for always believing in me. For asking, "What's next?" and helping me find a way through. Thank you for planting such important seeds so long ago that are still blooming and providing fruit. Who knew I would ever write a *book*? You. Thank you for the opportunities you have provided for me. Thank you for supporting me, loving me, and showering me with constant encouragement. Dad, thank you for being a deep, earthly grounding for me. Thank you for loving Mother Nature in important ways that continue to show up in my art. You are priceless.

Thank you to the "Lutheran Table" who planted the seed from the time I was little, talking about the book I would one day write about all your dysfunction. You planted the seed for the book; the content may have changed over time, but you planted the seed of "someday when you write a book..." Thank you to Susan B, Tom and Char, Bob and Pam, Steve and Teri, George and Tammie, Dave and Ann, and all you other crazy Lutherans who knew I'd write a book someday—years and years before I ever even considered it. Planting seeds is important. Thank you for tilling the soil and planting those seeds. Thank you for teaching me the importance of speaking words over others, as silly or serious as they may be.

Jessica B, thank you for holding my hand and being with me through the darkness. For being a light to lead the way. Thank you for your relationship, your trust, your encouragement, and your love. This book was birthed with you by my side. Thank you for encouraging me to trust, to believe, and to press on into the space of the deep, where people lurk alone and want so desperately to have a person. Thank you for being my person.

Jed S, thank you for sending your deep thoughts, your random ramblings, and your juicy goodness. It was such a gift for you to show up when I needed you, from whatever exotic place you were in at the time. Your commitment to me and this process has been so life-giving. I feel so honored you would walk this journey with me with such significant intention. I'm so thankful for you and your wisdom.

Aunt Kathy, thank you for your groundedness, and your quiet, slow, intentional reflections, all deeply rooted in the goodness of creation. In many ways, the progression of this book is a reflection of you and the love, longings, and ponderings you've shared with me. Thank you for showing up for me authentically and bravely you; it was just what I needed to do the same for my readers. I love you.

Thank you to Sherry D, Dana D, Esther C, Heather K, and Took S. You consistently showed up when I needed you, when I needed help, direction, and clarity. Your words were meaningful to keep me on the path. Thank you for reminding me of the important pieces along the way. Thank you, Liz J, for having the faith and courage to give me the word *create*.

There are so many people who have lived the content of this book with me. Without you, I would not have words to write and stories to tell. Thank you to my students, my interns, my supervisees, and my readers. You are some of the most beautiful people I have ever met. Thank you for showing up with great intention and vulnerability, for believing in the work I do, and for giving me the words to share with the world what it's like to be a learner.

Thank you to all the students who have gone with me along this journey, who have taught me so much about me and the work of a counselor. You inspire me, you challenge me, you motivate me, and you encourage me. Thank you.

Thank you to my Hope*Books cohort for walking this journey with me, encouraging me, crying with me, and being fellow journeyers with me. Thank you to Krissy Nelson and Brian Dixon at Hope*Media for believing in me, my words, and my story. Thank you for seeing the future of my book even before I could. Thank you for your authentic and driven support. And thank you to my editor, Abby McDonald, for reading, reviewing, editing, sifting, switching, scratching, cutting, and supporting. Wow. I'm so thankful there are people like you in this book creation process.

Thank you to the friends who challenge me to show up, be brave, and keep growing deeper: Brandon J, Mark P, Terra and Jeff Mattson, Gina P, Shelby C, Joy V, Deanna and Monica, Heidi T, Jazmin, Hailey, Dani, Nancy S, Frankie, Jordyn, Catherine G, Sarah F, Vivian H, Madeline B, Kelsey E, Richard and Karen, Heidi G, and Polly M.

To the countless scholars, teachers, mentors, gardeners, and creators who have gone before me. From my roots to my blooms, thank you.

Lord, all the walls are down and the idols exposed; I have nothing left to hide. I give You my last words because they all came from You, and there's nothing more beautiful and honoring than to be Your instrument. Thy will be done. Amen.

Notes

Part One - Burdened

1. Christine Caine [@ChristineCaine]. "Sometimes when you're in a dark place you think you've been buried, but you've actually been planted." *X*, 13 Aug. 2023, 8:49 a.m., https://twitter.com/ChristineCaine/status/1690752319275905024

Chapter 1 - Buried Under Books

1. Rowling, J. K., et al. *Harry Potter and the Sorcerer's Stone*. Scholastic Inc., 2023.

Chapter 2 - Ghosts in the Nursery

1. Tronick, Ed. Still Face Experiment. Zero to Three, 2007, https://www.youtube.com/watch?v=vmE3NfB_HhE

2. Fraiberg, Selma, et al. "Ghosts in the nursery." *Journal of the American Academy of Child Psychiatry*, vol. 14, no. 3, 1975, pp. 387–421, https://doi.org/10.1016/s0002-7138(09)61442-4.

3. Siegel, Daniel J. *Brainstorm. The Power and Purpose of the Teenage Brain*. Jeremy P. Tarcher/Penguin, 2013.

4. Hanson, Rick. *Hardwiring Happiness: The New Brain Science of Contentment, Calm, and Confidence*. Harmony Books, 2016.

5. Rosen, Michael, and Helen Oxenbury. *We're Going on a Bear Hunt*. Little Simon, 2009.

6. Perry, Bruce D., and Oprah Winfrey. *What Happened to You?: Conversations on Trauma, Resilience, and Healing*. Flatiron, 2021. Brandt, Kristie, and Bruce D Perry. *Infant and Early Childhood*

Mental Health Core Concepts and Clinical Practice. American Psychiatric Publ, 2014. Van der Kolk , Bessel. *The Body Keeps the Score: Brain, Mind and Body in the Healing of Trauma*. Penguin Books, 2015.

Siegel, Daniel J., and Marion F. Solomon. *Healing Trauma Attachment, Mind, Body, and Brain*. W. W. Norton & Company, 2003.

Chapter 3 - What the Hell am I Doing Here?

1. Freeman, Emily P. *A Million Little Ways: Uncover the Art You Were Made to Live*. Revell, a Division of Baker Publishing Group, 2013.

2. Johnson, Susan M. *The Practice of Emotionally Focused Couple Therapy: Creating Connection*. Routledge, Taylor & Francis Group, 2020.

Part Two - Becoming

1. Sue Monk Kidd. *The Dance of the Dissident Daughter : A Woman's Journey from Christian Tradition to the Sacred Feminine*. New York, N.Y., Harperone, 2007.

Chapter 4 - Lean into Love

1. Chapman, Gary D. *The 5 Love Languages: The Secret to Love That Lasts*. Northfield Publishing, 2015.

2. *Love Is Blind*. Created by Chris Coelen, season 1, Netflix, 13 Feb. 2020.

3. *The Bible*. Authorized King James Version, Oxford UP, 1998.

4. Nouwen, Henri. "Small Steps of Love." 15 June 2018, https://henrinouwen.org/meditations/small-steps-love. Accessed 1 Sep. 2023.

5. Wilder, Jim, and Dallas Willard. *Renovated: God, Dallas Willard & The Church That Transforms*. NavPress, 2020.

Chapter 5 - Created for Connection

1. Girls on the Run, girlsontherun.org

   From the website: Girls on the Run inspires participants of all abilities to recognize their individual strengths while building a sense of connection in a team setting. [...] At the end of the season, the team completes a 5K together, which provides a tangible sense of accomplishment and sets a confident mindset into motion.

2. Johnson, Susan M. *Attachment Theory in Practice: Emotionally Focused Therapy (EFT) with Individuals, Couples, and Families.* The Guilford Press, 2019.

3. Harlow, Harry F. "The nature of love." *American Psychologist*, vol. 13, no. 12, 1958, pp. 673–685, https://doi.org/10.1037/h0047884.

4. Lieberman, Alicia F., et al. "Angels in the nursery: The intergenerational transmission of benevolent parental influences." *Infant Mental Health Journal*, vol. 26, no. 6, 2005, pp. 504–520, https://doi.org/10.1002/imhj.20071.

Chapter 6 - Stop Pretending to be a Therapist

1. Quote by E.E. Cummings, unknown origins.

2. Spielberg, Steven, director. *Hook.* TriStar Pictures, 1991.

3. *Mister Rogers' Neighborhood.* Created by Fred Rogers, season 1, National Educational Television, 19 Feb. 1968.

4. Ramis, Harold, director. *Bedazzled.* 2000.

5. *The Magic School Bus.* Created by Joanna Cole, and Bruce Degen, season 1, PBS, 10 Sept. 1994.

6. Nouwen, Henri J. M. *Here and Now: Living in the Spirit.* Crossroad, 2001.

Chapter 7 - Stay in Your Lane

1. Psychotherapy.net hosts various videos with family therapy theorists and experts. This series is called "With the Experts."

2. Brown, Brené. *Daring Greatly: How the Courage to Be Vulnerable Transforms the Way We Live, Love, Parent and Lead.* Avery, 2015.

3. Kolber, Aundi. *Strong like Water: Finding the Freedom, Safety, & Compassion to Move through Hard Things--& Experience True Flourishing.* Tyndale Refresh, 2023.

4. Freeman, Emily P. *A Million Little Ways: Uncover the Art You Were Made to Live.* Revell, a Division of Baker Publishing Group, 2013.

5. Brencher, Hannah. *Fighting Forward: Your Nitty Gritty Guide to Beating the Lies That Hold You Back.* Zondervan, 2021.

Chapter 8 - Sacred Air

1. A quote attributed to the character Winnie the Pooh.

Chapter 9 - You First

1. Rowling, J. K., and Mary GrandPré. *Harry Potter and the Goblet of Fire.* Scholastic, 2002.

2. Kolber, Aundi. *Try Softer: A Fresh Approach to Move Us out of Anxiety, Stress, and Survival Mode-and into a Life of Connection and Joy.* Tyndale House Publishers, Inc., 2020.

Chapter 10 - Follow the Flight of Song

1. Taoist Proverb, unknown origins.

2. Longfellow, Henry Wadsworth. *The Belfry of Bruges, and Other Poems.* John Owen, 1846.

3. Jalal Al-Din Rumi, Maulana, et al. *The Essential Rumi.* Harperone, 2004.

4. "Encanto." Walt Disney Studios Home Entertainment, 2022.

5. Kolber, Aundi. *Try Softer: A Fresh Approach to Move Us out of Anxiety, Stress, and Survival Mode-and into a Life of Connection and Joy.* Tyndale House Publishers, Inc., 2020.

Chapter 11 - The Road Not Taken

1. Johnson, Susan M. *The Practice of Emotionally Focused Couple Therapy: Creating Connection.* Routledge, Taylor & Francis Group, 2020.

2. Frost, Robert. "The Road Not Taken." *The Atlantic Monthly*, Aug. 1915.

Chapter 12 - Listen Within

1. Freeman, Emily P., host. "Why Self-Care isn't Selfish with Taylor Elyse Morrison" *The Next Right Thing*, episode 276, emilypfreeman.com/podcast/276/. Accessed 1 Sept. 2023.

Chapter 12 - Fight Song

1. *Cauley, Lorinda Bryan. Goldilocks and the Three Bears. New York :Putnam, 1981.*

2. Enneagram, from the Enneagram Institute: https://www.enneagraminstitute.com/

Part Three - Belonging

1. Brené Brown. *Braving the Wilderness : The Quest for True Belonging and the Courage to Stand Alone.* New York, Random House, 2017.

Made in United States
Troutdale, OR
10/24/2024

24094957R00154